Library of
Davidson College

STEPHEN GILLERS is associate professor of law at New York University. After graduating from law school in 1968, he served as law clerk to Chief Judge Gus J. Solomon of the United States District Court in Oregon, and then entered private law practice in New York City, most recently with Warner and Gillers, P.C. He was executive director of the Society of American Law Teachers from 1973 to 1978. He has written numerous articles and written and edited a half dozen books on law and law-related subjects.

Also in this Series

THE RIGHTS OF VETERANS	36285	$1.75
THE RIGHTS OF MENTAL PATIENTS	36574	$1.75
THE RIGHTS OF MILITARY PERSONNEL	33365	$1.50
THE RIGHTS OF YOUNG PEOPLE	31963	$1.50
THE RIGHTS OF ALIENS	31534	$1.50
THE RIGHTS OF STUDENTS	32045	$1.50
THE RIGHTS OF MENTALLY RETARDED PERSONS	31351	$1.50
THE RIGHTS OF CANDIDATES AND VOTERS	28159	$1.50
THE RIGHTS OF GAY PEOPLE	24976	$1.75
THE RIGHTS OF GOVERNMENT EMPLOYEES	38505	$1.75
THE RIGHTS OF HOSPITAL PATIENTS	22459	$1.50
THE RIGHTS OF THE POOR	28002	$1.25
THE RIGHTS OF SUSPECTS	28043	$1.25
THE RIGHTS OF TEACHERS	25049	$1.50
THE RIGHTS OF WOMEN	27953	$1.75

Where better paperbacks are sold, or directly from the publisher. Include 25¢ per copy for mailing; allow three weeks for delivery.

Avon Books, Mail Order Dept., 250 West 55th Street, New York, N.Y. 10019

AN AMERICAN
CIVIL LIBERTIES
UNION HANDBOOK

THE RIGHTS OF LAWYERS AND CLIENTS

Stephen Gillers

General Editor of this series:
Norman Dorsen, *Chairperson*

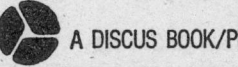

A DISCUS BOOK/PUBLISHED BY AVON BOOKS

THE RIGHTS OF LAWYERS AND CLIENTS is an original publication of Avon Books. This work has never before appeared in book form.

AVON BOOKS
A division of
The Hearst Corporation
959 Eighth Avenue
New York, New York 10019

Copyright © 1979 by the American Civil Liberties Union
Published by arrangement with the American Civil Liberties Union.
Library of Congress Catalog Card Number: 78-61701
ISBN: 0-380-42382-0

All rights reserved, which includes the right
to reproduce this book or portions thereof in
any form whatsoever. For information address
Avon Books.

First Discus Printing, February, 1979

DISCUS TRADEMARK REG. U.S. PAT. OFF. AND IN OTHER COUNTRIES, MARCA REGISTRADA, HECHO EN U.S.A.

Printed in the U.S.A.

Acknowledgments

I am especially grateful to Sheila Rossi for her contribution to the writing and research of this book. Early on, she assisted in the compilation of some of the information in the appendices, but by far her major and essential contribution was the careful and diligent check of every one of the thousand-odd cases cited here. She caught more mistakes than I care to admit. Her tenacity in pursuing the task, in all its intricate detail, makes me and every reader of this book indebted to her. Any errors that managed to slip by remain my responsibility.

I also wish to thank the following individuals for their work in putting this manuscript into appropriate form. Their work included everything from typing to arranging the appendices to cutting and pasting and all kinds of other mechanical and often boring tasks. They are Joan Altman, Lisa Zimmermann, Frances Hunt, and Joan Silber.

I would like to thank the Council for Public Interest Law for permission to use, in appendix B of this book, the list of federal statutes permitting the award of court-ordered attorneys' fees. The list comes from the Council's excellent study, *Balancing the Scales of Justice*. I also wish to thank the publication *Before the Bar* for permission to use some of the information in appendix A on residence and reciprocity requirements for admissions to the bars of various states.

It is a pleasure to dedicate this book to Morris Abram, Edward Costikyan, Arthur Liman, Martin London, and Jay Topkis, five lawyers who taught a new lawyer many valuable lessons about legal skills, and who, by their early example, continue to influence his professional growth.

Fond appreciation is due my former partner Kenneth E. Warner for the firm time and resources I used to write this book. He tolerated my effort as if it were for our best-paying client.

Finally, I owe a great debt to Judge Gus J. Solomon and to Professor James C. Kirby, Jr. of NYU Law School. Both contributed much time to reading drafts of the manuscript of this book, making valuable suggestions for improvement.

Stephen Gillers

Contents

Preface — xi

Introduction — xiii

I. Admission to the Bar — 19

II. Admission pro Haec Vice — 35

III. Lawyer Discipline — 43

IV. Lawyer Discipline—Some Procedural Issues — 71

V. The Attorney-Client Relationship — 81

VI. Conflicts of Interest — 103

VII. Attorneys' Fees and Attorneys' Liens — 117

VIII. Malpractice and Deals between Attorney and Client — 135

IX. Limits on Advocacy, Including First-Amendment Rights of Lawyers and Clients — 147

X. The Rights of Indigents, Clients Who Represent Themselves, and Non-lawyers Who Sell Law-Related Services — 173

Appendices — 181

Preface

This guide sets forth your rights under present law and offers suggestions on how you can protect your rights. It is one of a continuing series of handbooks published in cooperation with the American Civil Liberties Union.

The hope surrounding these publications is that Americans informed of their rights will be encouraged to exercise them. Through their exercise, rights are given life. If they are rarely used, they may be forgotten and violations may become routine.

This guide offers no assurances that your rights will be respected. The laws may change and, in some of the subjects covered in these pages, they change quite rapidly. An effort has been made to note those parts of the law where movement is taking place but it is not always possible to predict accurately when the law *will* change.

Even if the laws remain the same, interpretations of them by courts and administrative officials often vary. In a federal system such as ours, there is a built-in problem of the differences between state and federal law, not to speak of the confusion of the differences from state to state. In addition, there are wide variations in the ways in which particular courts and administrative officials will interpret the same law at any given moment.

If you encounter what you consider to be a specific abuse of your rights you should seek legal assistance. There are a number of agencies that may help you, among them ACLU affiliate offices, but bear in mind that the

ACLU is a limited-purpose organization. In many communities, there are federally funded legal service offices which provide assistance to poor persons who cannot afford the costs of legal representation. In general, the rights that the ACLU defends are freedom of inquiry and expression; due process of law; equal protection of the laws; and privacy. The authors in this series have discussed other rights in these books (even though they sometimes fall outside the ACLU's usual concern) in order to provide as much guidance as possible.

These books have been planned as guides for the people directly affected: therefore the question and answer format. In some of these areas there are more detailed works available for "experts." These guides seek to raise the largest issues and inform the non-specialist of the basic law on the subject. The authors of the books are themselves specialists who understand the need for information at "street level."

No attorney can be an expert in every part of the law. If you encounter a specific legal problem in an area discussed in one of these handbooks, show the book to your attorney. Of course, he will not be able to rely *exclusively* on the handbook to provide you with adequate representation. But if he hasn't had a great deal of experience in the specific area, the handbook can provide helpful suggestions on how to proceed.

> Norman Dorsen, Chairperson
> American Civil Liberties Union

The principal purpose of these handbooks is to inform individuals of their rights. The authors from time to time suggest what the law should be. When this is done, the views expressed are not necessarily those of the American Civil Liberties Union.

Introduction

When I started work on this book, it was going to be called *The Rights of Lawyers*. Some people were puzzled: "You mean lawyers have rights?" they asked. Others were annoyed. "Why don't you write about the rights of clients?" they said. "Lawyers have too many rights."

Often, when you come to the limits of a right, you run up against a responsibility. So in writing about the rights of lawyers, I discovered I could not avoid (and did not want to avoid) the rights of those they serve. Their clients. The title of the book changed accordingly.

"Oh, you're *just* writing a book about legal ethics," came the next batch of replies, mainly from lawyers, when they heard the new title of the book. No, I answered. "But how can you write about the rights of clients without writing about the ethics of lawyers?" I was asked.

The answer is you can and you can't. If that answer sounds like it came from a lawyer, well, it did. But it's the right answer. A study of the rights of lawyers and clients covers some issues that also concern legal ethics, but from a different perspective, and covers much other material that has little to do with ethics. The right to be admitted to the bar, disciplinary procedures, attorneys' liens and fees, authority, malpractice, and the attorney-client privilege are subjects that all go well beyond a study of ethics. Even problems raised in the area of conflicts of interests, though springing from provisions of the Code of Professional Responsibility (discussed in Chapters III and VI), have sources and implications apart from conventionally ethical ones. In short, for the most part, the rights and responsibilities discussed here have their genesis in many places other than the Code—in case law, statutes, customs, the Constitution, court rules, and so on.

Someone who works daily in a law office knows that the profession is changing in ways not yet fully understood. The last quarter-century has seen remarkable developments in substantive law. Whole new fields have been created— environmental law, poverty law, women's rights. But today, we are faced with imminent changes in a different area of law, which will perhaps have a more fundamental effect on our social structure. We are changing the ways in which we apply law and distribute legal services.

We are changing, for example, the ways lawyers are taught, the bar is organized, discipline occurs, clients get represented, legal services are delivered, and disputes are settled. And while I cannot say what ultimate effect these changes will have, I can say what some of the causes are.

The constitutional protection for legal advertising, provided by the 1977 *Bates* decision, is only a beginning. Marketing people are already peddling creative ways for lawyers to get their message across, and even *The New York Times* has sent solicitations to lists of lawyers to advertise in its new legal-services columns.

But the movement will go beyond advertising—first, to solicitation; whispering that word would have brought punishment only a few years ago. Now the Supreme Court has decided two solicitation cases (one in favor of the lawyer) (see Chapter IX), and the Illinois Supreme Court has also had to deal with the issue (Chapter IX, again). And more. Recently I was called by a tenant organization and asked to make a "bid" on a test case the group wanted to bring. Other lawyers were bidding. The tenants would accept the lowest bid consistent with high quality. In connection with my bid, I was also to present my legal strategy. I told the fellow who called me that, while I was not interested for other reasons, I applauded the idea of consumer groups getting bids from lawyers. It will increase.

At the insistence of nonlawyers and a few lawyers, there has been much talk and a little experimentation with applying insurance principles to the delivery of legal services. Call it what you will—judicare, group practice—it spreads the risk of legal costs. Naturally, the organized bar has resisted this development, hiding behind apparently neutral ethical provisions, while really worrying about its collective pocketbook. "We can't do that," the bar says, "we're a profession not an . . . ugh . . . business." Of course, this is a lie. The practice of law is as much a business as anything else, and any lawyer who thinks it isn't will not be in business very long. The idea of legal insurance will not go away and will, I believe, continue to affect the structure of the profession and the delivery of legal service well into the twenty-first century.

Other developments that have the effect of spreading the risk or reducing the cost of legal services are legal clinics and lay organizations that buy legal talent wholesale. With regard to the latter, the Supreme Court provided such efforts with First Amendment protection beginning in the late 1960s. The first is just getting off the ground after years of being stymied—by ethical arguments—when the real issue has always been money. As ethical rules change—or the courts refuse to enforce them—thereby permitting high-volume, routine services to be delivered through legal clinics, many more people will be seeing lawyers than ever before. And more cheaply, because volume reduces the per-client overhead cost.

We don't need statistics on how the lawyer population has doubled in the last so many years to tell us that there are many more lawyers around than ever. Take this test. Listen in on a conversation on the bus or subway or in a restaurant. If you live in a large city, odds are that at least once a day you will hear someone talking about law—". . . so we made a motion to stay . . . ," ". . . the FTC's position in court was . . . ," ". . . my civil procedure exam is . . . ," and so on. Try this other test. Open a large city phone book and look down any column of names. At least one name in the column, more likely than not, will have "atty" after it. I have tried this on the Manhattan phone book and have yet to find a column with no attorney listed in it. We're being overrun by lawyers. The rapid increase in the number of LL.B.s and J.D.s cannot fail to affect the profession in ways too difficult to comprehend quite yet.

THE RIGHTS OF LAWYERS AND CLIENTS

If it is too soon to know what effect advertising, solicitation, "bidding" on legal services, insurance principles, the large increase in the number of lawyers, and the advent of clinics will have on the "rights" of lawyers and clients, at least the rights both groups have today are fairly clear. The chapters of this book try to explain them.

Chapter I deals with issues surrounding admission to the bar. Covered in this chapter are such questions as an applicant's right to see his or her exam paper, the possibility of court review of an examination, the legality of loyalty oaths, the legality of inquiry into associational memberships of the applicant, questions concerning character committees, the power to exclude applicants who have been convicted of a crime, residency requirements for admission, reciprocity admission, and the ability to become a lawyer without going to law school.

Chapter II reviews issues in a related area of admission to practice: *pro haec vice* admissions, or the right of a lawyer admitted in State A to try a case or give advice in State B. This is a developing area of the law, with much activity and changing attitudes. I believe it will change more, in favor of expanded rights of *pro haec vice* admission, as the concept of a national bar continues to develop.

Chapters III and IV deal with lawyer discipline. Chapter III is mainly concerned with grounds for disciplining a lawyer, but also covers certain fundamental procedural issues, such as the confidentiality of disciplinary proceedings. Chapter III also reviews such questions as the power to discipline, reinstatement, the effect of criminal convictions, discipline for incompetence or neglect, discipline for the conduct of one's partner or associate, discipline of prosecutors, discipline and double jeopardy, suspension for mental illness, and the relevance of a lawyer's purely private life on his right to practice law. Chapter IV continues with some special procedural issues, such as the constitutional rights at a disciplinary hearing, the burden of proof, presumptions, the relationship between disciplinary proceedings and the privilege against self-incrimination, federal intervention into state disciplinary proceedings, and discipline in retaliation for the exercise of First Amendment rights.

Chapter V reviews the attorney-client relationship, in-

INTRODUCTION

cluding the attorney-client privilege, the nature of a lawyer's fiduciary relation to his client, the obligation of a client to the lawyer, the authority of the attorney to act for the client and limits on that authority, ways in which the attorney-client relationship can end, and the power of the client to act against his attorney's advice.

The issue of conflict of interest, discussed in Chapter VI, raises many questions. Among them is the ability of a lawyer to take on a representation if it involves putting himself in an adversary relation to a former client. When is this allowed and when is it prohibited? An incidental issue is the right of a former government lawyer to represent interests that concerned him while he was in government employ. Can an attorney sue a current client? If an attorney is disqualified from a representation, what about his partners, associates, and officemates? Can clients with conflicting interests agree to be represented by the same lawyer?

Attorneys' fees and attorneys' liens are the subjects of Chapter VII. How are fees determined? When are contingent fees not allowed? When can a client get his opponent to pay his lawyer? Can a client ever get money back after he has paid his lawyer? What if the client fires the lawyer or the lawyer quits during the representation? The chapter concludes with a discussion of the different forms of attorneys' liens and how they may vary from state to state.

Chapter VIII mainly deals with issues of attorney malpractice, the level of skill an attorney must bring to a representation, the liability of lawyers to persons other than immediate clients, the problem of the attorney who acquires an interest adverse to the interests of his client, lawyers and clients who enter into business deals together, and gifts from client to lawyer.

Chapter IX deals with a collection of issues which I have called "Limits on Advocacy, Including First Amendment Rights of Lawyers and Clients." Among the many issues discussed here are questions about how far a lawyer can go in representing and protecting the interests of his client, including, for example, whether he can advise a client to disobey a court order. Also discussed in Chapter IX is the question of the right of lawyers to criticize the courts generally or particular judges. Issues of advertising and solicitation are discussed in Chapter IX, as are the First Amendment rights of clients to organize to gain cheaper access to the courts. The chapter concludes with a discussion of the power of the courts to control the dress and appearance of lawyers and clients.

Finally, Chapter X discusses the rights of clients who represent themselves, including the rights of nonlawyers to sell law-related services such as "divorce-yourself" kits. Chapter X also discusses some of the rights of indigent criminal defendants with respect to counsel.

Throughout the book, there are many issues that could have been shifted from one chapter to another as, indeed, there are many issues discussed in more than one place. I have found, in writing this book, that the sources of rights for lawyers and clients are plentiful, and that rights issues can arise in many ways. As the questions I received as I was writing this book indicate, not many people think of lawyers and clients as having rights in the affirmative sense —but in fact those rights constitute the bedrock of our legal system and are essential to its capacity to perform justly.

    Stephen Gillers
    January 1, 1979

I
Admission to the Bar

Who determines the standards for admission to the bar of a state—the legislature or the courts?

Both. The situation differs from state to state, but usually the state legislature will pass a broad authorizing statute enabling the courts, generally the highest court in the state, to specify rules for the admission and discipline of lawyers.[1] Sometimes a state's constitution contains a provision giving the courts of the state power to determine standards for admission to the bar.[2] Courts have not been reluctant to strike down legislation that infringes on this power.[3] Some courts have ruled that they have "inherent power" to admit and discipline lawyers, without any need for a state constitutional provision or statute granting it.[4]

Will the courts review a determination by state bar examiners that an applicant to the bar failed to pass the examination required for admission?

The courts will generally not review such determinations.[5] At best, courts in some states will review an applicant's bar examination only if the applicant can show that his or her failure was a result of fraud or coercion or imposition by the bar examiners.[6] In other states, the standard for review is whether the determination was arbitrary, capricious, or an abuse of discretion.[7]

Does an applicant to the bar who fails a written qualifying examination have a right to see his or her examination paper?

In some states, an applicant does have such a right under state rules or statutes.[8]

Where a state statute or rule does not provide such a right, does the constitutional right to due process of law require it anyway?

Only one court has held that it does. The Supreme Court of Alaska ruled that an unsuccessful applicant is entitled to see his or her examination, model answers, and the examination questions. The applicant should also receive a "representative sampling of the examination papers of other applicants who received overall passing and overall failing grades."[9] Other courts, however, have ruled that there is no constitutional right to see one's bar examination.[10]

How free is the state to structure the questions on the bar examination?

As long as the state is not arbitrary and does not violate a constitutional right or act with a constitutionally impermissible reason, the state is free to structure a bar exam as it chooses. It can use essay questions if it wants. It can make its bar examination more comprehensive and more difficult than those in other states.[11]

Will the courts ever review the substantive fairness of bar-examination questions?

Rarely, but it did happen in one case. A federal district judge ordered federal examiners who administered tests to persons who wished to practice before the Patent Office to give credit to an applicant on a particular question. The question carried a potential ten points of credit. The applicant had received no credit for his answer. The court, after doing its own research, concluded that there was no clear-cut answer to the question, and that it was therefore "clearly erroneous" to deny the applicant any credit at all. But the judge did not say how much credit the applicant should receive for his answer to the question.[12]

Will a court order bar examiners to admit a failing applicant on the ground that the test scores were computed and the passing grades determined in a statistically unfair manner?

Very rarely. One court did so after the applicants were able to show that persons receiving lower grades had passed the exam and the bar examiners could not satisfactorily explain the discrepancy, but that court's decision was later overturned on the ground that the comparisons were of exams given in different years, among other differences.[13]

Is a state's bar examination subject to attack on the ground that a substantially higher percentage of whites taking the exam pass than blacks?

No. The mere fact that a higher percentage of one race passes the exam than do members of another race will not invalidate a state's bar examination. This is true even if the difference is four times as great or greater. The bar examination only need be rationally related to the state's valid interest in licensing professionals. The fact that the exam has a disparate racial impact will not invalidate it. Nor does it matter that a state's bar exam does not comport with the standards for educational and psychological tests published by the American Psychological Association.[14]

Can an applicant to the bar be required to take an oath?

It depends upon what the oath says. An applicant can be required to swear or affirm that he or she will support the state and federal constitutions.[15] On the other hand, an oath that includes the phrase "So help me God" has been held an infringement on the free exercise of religion.[16] Aliens cannot be excluded from admission to the bar of a state on the theory that they cannot pledge allegiance to the United States.[17]

THE RIGHTS OF LAWYERS AND CLIENTS

Can an applicant be denied admission because of his or her beliefs or the associations to which he or she may have belonged?

No. In two cases in 1971, the Supreme Court ruled that the First Amendment prohibits a state from excluding a person from the bar solely because of the applicant's membership in a political organization or because of the applicant's political beliefs. In one case, the applicant refused to tell the character committee whether she had ever belonged to an organization that advocated the overthrow of the United States government by force or violence. Four justices held that this question could not constitutionally be asked. One justice, concurring, believed that the question was unacceptable because it did not limit itself to an inquiry about "knowing membership" in such an organization.[18] In another case, the applicant answered all questions put to him by the Ohio authorities, but declined to answer questions (a) inquiring whether he had ever been a member of an organization that advocated the overthrow of the United States government by force, (b) asking for a list of all organizations of which he had ever been a member, and (c) asking for a list of all organizations he had joined since becoming a law student. Five justices ruled these questions unconstitutional.[19]

Can a state condition admission to its bar on the character of the applicant?

Yes. But the character test must be fairly restricted. As a general matter, the state cannot exclude applicants because of what they believe or how they choose to lead their purely private lives. The inquiry into the applicant's character must be narrow and only relate to qualities a state may properly require from an applicant to its bar.[20]

What are some examples of character traits that can keep an applicant out of the bar?

In one case, the state character committee obtained the applicant's Selective Service file. This file contained a psychiatric evaluation of the applicant, which indicated that he was "unacceptable for induction because of a moderately severe character defect manifested by well-documented ideation with a paranoid flavor and grandiose character." The applicant, furthermore, declined a request by the character committee that he take a psychiatric examination. The court ruled that it was not improper for the character committee to obtain a copy of the psychiatric report and that the report was properly considered by the committee in reaching its conclusion to deny admission. The committee was upheld.[21]

So an applicant's mental condition is validly part of the character inquiry?

Yes. In another case, a special committee recommended that an applicant not be permitted to sit for the bar examination because he suffered from an "established personality disorder of a character and pattern which will persist in the event the applicant is admitted to the practice of law." The committee concluded that the "disorder" caused the applicant to be "unreasonably suspicious that bad motives and intentions activate persons with whom he comes into contact," causes him "to make irresponsible and highly derogatory untrue public accusations," and "causes him to bring and pursue with great persistence groundless claims in court proceedings and otherwise." Although the court in this case recognized that the practice of law "is not a privilege but a right," the right was held to be conditioned upon the applicant having "the necessary mental, physical, and moral qualifications." After reviewing the record, the court also concluded that the applicant had "failed to demonstrate that he is mentally able to engage in the active and continuous practice of law."[22]

How about people convicted of criminal activity?

It is almost impossible to be admitted to the bar of any state if the applicant has been convicted of a felony. Some states expressly disqualify convicted felons in their statutory law.[23] There are rare exceptions, as in the case of Alger Hiss, who had been convicted of perjury during the McCarthy period (although he always maintained his innocence) and was recently readmitted to the bar of the state of Massachusetts.[24] Misdemeanor convictions, on the other hand, will not automatically result in disqualification. Rather the inquiry is whether the particular crime involved moral turpitude. In one case, the fact that an applicant had been convicted of several misdemeanors and had, as a youth, engaged in fistfights, was held not sufficient to justify a denial of admission to practice.[25] In another case, a petit larceny conviction was held not to automatically exclude an applicant from admission. In the same case, the court ruled that even where an applicant had been convicted of a felony, a subsequent pardon would remove her disqualification for admission.[26]

What other reasons might a state have to deny admission to an applicant based on character?

Giving false statements to material questions on the application,[27] knowing disregard of the truth,[28] and the failure to register for the draft until more than seven years after an applicant's eighteenth birthday[29] were each considered grounds for denial of admission. On the other hand, driving under the influence of an intoxicating beverage was not, standing alone, judged enough to evince a lack of good moral character.[30]

If an applicant has been convicted of a crime but his or her conviction has been expunged under applicable law, can a state body considering the applicant's admission nevertheless require the applicant to reveal the conviction?

At least one court has held that it can. The court noted that while information regarding expunged offenses is not "necessarily determinative of the moral character of an applicant," it is relevant. The applicant did not have a constitutional right to withhold the information.[31] The Supreme Court affirmed.

Is an applicant who is denied admission because of his or her character entitled to a hearing?

Yes, the applicant is entitled to a hearing somewhere along the way. The hearing includes the right to present one's own side of the story and the right of confrontation.[32] The hearing can be held either before an administrative body that inquires into character and fitness or before a reviewing court.[33]

ADMISSION TO THE BAR

Will a court review the determination of a character committee?

It depends on the state. Most courts will review such determinations to some extent. One court has held that it will not reverse a determination of its Board of Law Examiners if there is substantial evidence in the record supporting the conclusion.[34] Other courts have stressed that the findings of the bar examiners are not binding upon the court, though they may be entitled to great weight with the burden on the applicant to show that the board's determination was erroneous. Reasonable doubts should be resolved in favor of the applicant.[35]

Who has the burden of proving or disproving good moral character?

The applicant bears the burden of showing his good moral character.[36]

What if an applicant to the bar has been previously charged with a crime, but the criminal proceeding terminated in his favor?

The underlying facts can still be considered by the bar examiners and can constitute sufficient reason for denying admission. In one case, an applicant had been charged with incitement to riot as a result of certain speeches he made during a student demonstration. He was acquitted. Nevertheless, the bar examiners declined to admit him. They concluded that his explanation of the underlying facts was false and had been advanced solely to deceive the examiners. The Supreme Court of California reversed, holding, among other things, that the denial of certification in such a case can be upheld only if it was concluded *beyond any reasonable doubt* that the applicant's version not only was objectively false but had been advanced by him with an intent to deceive the committee.[37]

Can the state deny an applicant admission to the bar based on secret or confidential information about the applicant's character?

No, at least not if the denial is based "solely" on this information. The applicant must be given a chance to contest the evidence against her.[38]

THE RIGHTS OF LAWYERS AND CLIENTS

If an applicant has been guilty of some misconduct in the past, does the length of time between the misconduct and the time he or she is seeking admission to the bar carry any weight?

Yes. At least one court has emphasized that the applicant's *present* character is the point at issue. "What the character had formerly been is relevant only as it blends with the continuous web of life and tinges its present texture." In this case, the fifty-six-year-old applicant had been involved in several minor criminal episodes, largely as a result of his use of alcohol. The most recent was seven years before the court decision.[39]

What are other examples of conduct found not to constitute bad moral character?

Each case, of course, depends heavily on its own facts. But in one leading Supreme Court decision, the facts that an applicant had used aliases for several years, though not for the purpose of cheating or defrauding; that he had been arrested, though not convicted; and that he had been a member of the Communist party for eight years, did not alone or in combination justify a denial of admission to the bar.[40] Chapter III contains additional "lifestyle" and sexual preference cases.

Can a state exclude a person from admission to its bar because he or she is not an American citizen?

No. The Supreme Court has ruled that alienage may not be a reason to exclude an applicant for admission to the bar of a state.[41]

May a state condition admission to its bar on a requirement that an applicant be a graduate of an accredited law school?

Yes.[42] In one case, an applicant was unable to obtain his degree from an acceptable law school because his prelegal education, although acceptable to the state bar, did not satisfy the law school's own degree requirements. Since the applicant could still go back and make up his prelaw work, the rule requiring a degree from a qualified law school before an applicant could be admitted to the state bar was held not to violate the Constitution.[43]

ADMISSION TO THE BAR

Do some states allow law-school graduates who are not members of the bar in any other state to be admitted without taking the bar examination?

Yes, some states have a "diploma privilege," under which graduates of that state's law schools are excused from taking the bar examination. Graduates of out-of-state law schools do not, however, enjoy this privilege.

Is this constitutional?
Yes.[44]

Which states have a diploma privilege?
Apparently, the only states that now have a diploma privilege are Mississippi, Montana, South Dakota, West Virginia, and Wisconsin.

Once a person is admitted to the bar of a state, can he be treated differently from other members of that state's bar?
Yes. In one case, Kansas divided its practitioners into two categories—those who were members of the Kansas bar and practiced in Kansas, and those who were members of the Kansas bar but were also members of the bar of other states where they regularly practiced. Attorneys in the second category were required to hire local Kansas counsel before they could appear in the courts of Kansas. This distinction was upheld.[45]

Can a state limit admission to its bar to applicants who are residents of the state?
Yes. A number of states once required lengthy residences before an applicant could be admitted to the state bar. For example, a residence requirement of a year or longer was not rare. These requirements have been struck down.[46] On the other hand, a state can require that an applicant be or intend to be a resident of the state at the time he or she takes the bar exam or applies for admission.[47] A six-month residence requirement for admission after the applicant has passed the bar exam has been upheld.[48] Appendix A lists the residence requirements of the various states.

THE RIGHTS OF LAWYERS AND CLIENTS

What about reciprocity?

Some states do have provisions under which they will admit an attorney who is already admitted in another state. Some states will admit such attorneys only if the state in which the attorney is already admitted grants its lawyers similar reciprocity.[49] Other states, like California, while not granting reciprocity, will allow attorneys to take a shorter or "attorney's" bar exam. A summary of the reciprocity provisions of each state is located in Appendix A.

What is an example of a state rule granting admission to members of a bar of another state without requiring them to take the bar examination?

The New York rule is one of the broadest; it opens the state bar to a person who (a) has been admitted to practice before the bar of another state or territory of the United States (or the District of Columbia), or (b) has been admitted to practice "as an attorney and counselor-at-law or the equivalent in the highest court of another country whose jurisprudence is based upon the principles of the English Common Law." There are other requirements. The attorney must have "actually practiced for a period of at least five years" in the highest law court or the highest court of original jurisdiction of the state or territory or common-law country where he is admitted. There are alternate ways to satisfy this provision if the applicant has practiced in the military or as counsel or assistant counsel in a corporation. An applicant can also have the bar examination waived if she graduated from an approved law school and has been teaching for five years at an American Bar Association–approved school located in the United States or one of its territories. In the latter case, the applicant must have obtained the rank of professor or associate professor. For all these exceptions, the applicant has to be at least twenty-six years of age and have been living in New York not less than six months.[50]

Where a state's reciprocity rule requires that the applicant, in order to be admitted without examination, have "been engaged in the actual practice of law" for a minimum period of time prior to his application, what must the applicant show?

28

Different courts have had different responses. In one Connecticut case, the applicant had been a member of the New York bar for some sixteen years, and for twelve of those years he had worked in a large New York firm. His duties required him to advise and assist "clients of the law firm on the merits, strategy, and conduct of the defense or suit and on settlement." He also had "responsibility for the direction of litigation, worked on briefs and questions of law, and participated in settlement discussions." However, since he was not a member of the litigation department of the firm, he never appeared in court. The Connecticut court interpreted the state rule to require that the applicant have "actually" practiced in the courtroom. Admission without examination was denied.

On the other hand, the New Mexico Supreme Court permitted an applicant to be admitted without examination where he had worked, for six years prior to application, for various government agencies. Only about 30 percent of the work he did actually required a law degree. He had never appeared in court. Nevertheless, the examination was waived. It is noteworthy that in New Mexico, the rule did not, as in Connecticut, require that the applicant have "actually practiced" law, but only that he have been in the full-time and continuous practice of law.

Finally, in a Rhode Island case, an applicant was not permitted to avoid the examination where his "practice" was in the legal department of a large corporation.[51]

Does it ever happen that a member of the bar of a foreign nation is admitted to the bar of a state without taking the bar examination?

Yes. As noted, some states, including New York, recognize attorneys who are members of the bar of foreign nations if the jurisprudence of those nations is based on the principles of English Common Law. In one case, an applicant who had been a member of the bar of Pakistan for the requisite period of time was ordered admitted without examination to the bar of the state of New York.[52]

Are there any states in which a person can qualify to take the bar examination without going to law school?

Yes. At one time it was not unusual for a person to

qualify to take a bar examination (or even to practice without examination) simply by working in a law office for a minimum period. Today, only California, Mississippi, Vermont, Virginia, and Washington state permit a person to take the bar exam after law-office study. But a number of other states allow an applicant to qualify to take the bar exam after some study inside a law school and the balance in a law office, without ever getting a law degree; these are, in addition to the five states just mentioned, Maine, New York, Texas, and Wyoming. This information can be found in a periodical publication of the Section of Legal Education of the American Bar Association entitled *Law School and Bar Admission Requirements*. This useful booklet also contains much other information on the requirements for admission to the bar of many states and information on virtually every law school in the nation. Single copies are available free by writing to the ABA at 1155 East Sixtieth Street, Chicago, Illinois 60637.

Will an attorney who gains admission to a state bar as a result of a "diploma privilege," or after studying law in a law office without going to law school for a degree, be able to gain admission to the bar of another state through reciprocity?

It depends on the rule of the other state. If the rule requires a bar examination, then the "diploma privilege" attorney will not be able to gain admission by reciprocity. Similarly, if the rule requires graduation from an accredited law school, then an attorney who qualified to take the bar exam in the first state only by studying law in a law office will not be able to gain admission. In other words, people who take advantage of the "diploma privilege" or who qualify to take a state bar examination without going to law school may find themselves barred from admission to a new state based on reciprocity.[53]

Can a state treat those who become members of its bar through reciprocity differently from those who take the the bar examination?

Yes. One state required that attorneys admitted through reciprocity must be permanent residents of the state and

ADMISSION TO THE BAR

intend to practice there as full-time members of the state bar. Attorneys who passed the bar exam, however, did not have the same requirement. This distinction was upheld as constitutional.[54]

Must a state give any kind of preference, such as an attorney's bar examination or reciprocity recognition, to a member of the bar of another state?
No.[55]

Can a state bar examiner require that practitioners (from other states) of long standing pass the same examination as is given to a recent law graduate?
Yes.[56]

Are there any privileges granted to a law-school graduate who goes into the armed services before taking the bar exam?
Sometimes. Local state rules will have to be checked, but some states do grant such a privilege. In New York, a person who goes into the armed services for more than one year after completing two years of law school and who satisfies certain New York residency requirements, can have the requirement of taking the bar exam dispensed with. But he or she must still complete the degree requirements at an approved law school. Likewise, a student who completes the degree requirements at an approved law school and then goes into the service, who spends more than one year there, and who misses the next two bar examinations after graduation because of active service can also have the examination requirement dispensed with.[57]

NOTES

1. N.Y. JUD. LAW §90 (McKinney).
2. *In re* Houston, 378 P.2d 644 (Alas. 1963); *in re* Steelman, 448 P.2d 817 (Alas. 1969) (by implication, but court will accept reasonable legislative standards).

3. Bd. of Comm'rs of the Ala. State Bar v. Baxley, 295 Ala. 100, 324 So.2d 256 (1975).
4. Graham v. Washington State Bar Ass'n., 86 Wash.2d 624, 548 P.2d 310 (1976); Belmont v. Board of Law Examiners, —— Tenn. ——, 511 S.W.2d 461 (1974); in re Feingold, 296 A.2d 492 (Me. 1972).
5. In re Peterson, 459 P.2d 703 (Alas. 1969).
6. Salot v. State Bar of Cal., 3 Cal.2d 615, 45 P.2d 203 (1935); Staley v. State Bar of Cal., 17 Cal.2d 119, 109 P.2d 667 (1941); in re Heaney, 106 Ariz. 391, 476 P.2d 846 (1970); in re Pacheco, 85 N.M. 600, 514 P.2d 1297 (1973); in re DeOrsey, 112, R.I. 536, 312 A.2d 720 (1973).
7. Davidson v. New York State Bd. of Law Examiners, 86 Misc. 2d 744, 382 N.Y.S.2d 418 (Sup. Ct. Albany County 1976); in re Wayland, 510 P.2d 1385 (Okla. 1971); in re Mead, —— Mass. ——, 361 N.E.2d 403 (1977), cert. denied, 434 U.S. 858 (Oct. 3, 1977).
8. Rules of the New York State Court of Appeals, §600.6. See Davidson, supra note 7, at 418, 421.
9. In re Peterson, supra note 5, at 703, 709.
10. Whitfield v. Illinois Bd. of Law Examiners, 504 F.2d 474 (7th Cir. 1974); Mrotek v. Nair, 4 Conn. Cir. Ct. 313, 231 A.2d 95 (1967).
11. Chaney v. State Bar of Cal., 386 F.2d 962 (9th Cir. 1967), cert. denied, 390 U.S. 1011 (1968); Whitfield, supra note 10; in re Mead, supra note 7.
12. Moran v. Tegemeyer, 363 F. Supp. 377 (D.D.C. 1973).
13. Richardson v. McFadden 540 F.2d 744 (4th Cir. 1976), reh en banc, 563 F.2d 1130 (4th Cir. 1977).
14. Pettit v. Gingerich, 427 F. Supp. 282 (D. Md. 1977). Cf. Washington v. Davis, 426 U.S. 229 (1976) (test for police valid although disproportionate number of minority-group members failed).
15. Law Students Civil Rights Research Council, Inc. v. Wadmond, 401 U.S. 154 (1971).
16. Nicholson v. Board of Comm'rs of Ala. State Bar Ass'n, 338 F. Supp 48 (D.C. Ala. 1972).
17. Raffaelli v. Committee of Bar Examiners, 7 Cal.3d 288, 496 P.2d 1264, 101 Cal. Rptr. 896 (1972).
18. Baird v. State Bar of Ariz., 401 U.S. 1 (1971).
19. In re Stolar, 401 U.S. 23 (1971).
20. Law Students Civil Rights Research Council, supra note 15; Hackin v. Lockwood, 361 F.2d 499 (9th Cir. 1966), cert. denied, 385 U.S. 960 (1966); Chaney, supra note 11.
21. Martin-Trigona v. Underwood, 529 F.2d 33 (7th Cir. 1975).

ADMISSION TO THE BAR

22. *In re* Ronwin, 113 Ariz. 357, 555 P.2d 315 (1976), *cert. denied*, 430 U.S. 917 (1977). The court disagreed with the committee's conclusion that the making of derogatory untrue public accusations should, in itself, be a ground to deny admission. It concluded that there was a good-faith belief in the merit of the accusations.
23. Rule 204, Colorado Rules Governing Admission to the Bar.
24. *In re* Hiss, —— Mass. ——, 333 N.E.2d 429 (1975).
25. Hallinan v. Committee of Bar Examiners of the State Bar of Cal., 65 Cal.2d 447, 421 P.2d 76, 55 Cal. Rptr. 228 (1966).
26. *In re* Florida Bd. of Bar Examiners, 183 So.2d 688 (Fla. 1966).
27. *In re* Bowen, 84 Nev. 681, 447 P.2d 658 (1968).
28. *In re* Capace, 110 R.I. 254, 291 A.2d 632 (1972).
29. *In re* Walker, 112 Ariz. 134, 539 P.2d 891 (1975).
30. *In re* Willis, 288 N.C. 1, 215 S.E.2d 771 (1975).
31. Wilson v. Wilson, 416 F. Supp. 984, 986 (D. Or. 1976) (three-judge court), *aff'd*, 430 U.S. 925 (1977).
32. Willner v. Committee on Character and Fitness, 373 U.S. 96 (1963).
33. *Ibid.*
34. *In re* Willis, *supra* note 30.
35. Bernstein v. Committee of Bar Examiners, 69 Cal.2d 90, 443 P.2d 570, 70 Cal. Rptr. 106 (1968).
36. Siegel v. Committee of Bar Examiners, 10 Cal.3d 156, 514 P.2d 967 110 Cal. Rptr. 15 (1973).
37. *Ibid.* (emphasis in the original) For further cases on the burden of proof, the rights of the applicant before the bar examiners, and the degree of review before the courts, *see in re* Warren, 149 Conn. 266, 178 A.2d 528 (1962); *in re* Dinan, 157 Conn. 67, 244 A.2d 608 (1968).
38. *In re* Burke, 87 Ariz. 336, 351 P.2d 169 (1960); *in re* Guberman, 90 Ariz. 27, 363 P.2d 617 (1961).
39. *In re* Monaghan, 126 Vt. 53, 65, 222 A.2d 665, 675 (1966).
40. Schware v. Board of Bar Examiners of N.M., 353 U.S. 232 (1957); *see also* Konigsberg v. State Bar of Cal., 353 U.S. 252 (1957).
41. *In re* Griffiths, 413 U.S. 717 (1973).
42. Hackin, *supra* note 20.
43. Lombardi v. Tauro, 470 F.2d 798 (1st Cir. 1972), *cert. denied*, 412 U.S. 919 (1973).
44. Shenfield v. Prather, 387 F. Supp. 676 (N.D. Miss. 1974); Huffman v. Montana Supreme Court, 372 F. Supp. 1175 (D. Mont. 1974), *aff'd* 419 U.S. 955 (1974).

45. Martin v. Walton, 368 U.S. 25 (1961).
46. Smith v. Davis, 350 F. Supp. 1225 (S.D.W. Va. 1972); Webster v. Wofford, 321 F. Supp. 1259 (N.D. Ga. 1970).
47. Wilson, *supra* note 31.
48. Tang v. Appellate Division of N.Y. Supreme Court, 373 F. Supp. 800 (S.D.N.Y. 1972), *aff'd*, 487 F.2d 138 (1973), *cert. denied*, 416 U.S. 906 (1974).
49. Goldsmith v. Pringle, 399 F. Supp. 620 (D. Colo. 1975).
50. Rules of the New York State Court of Appeals, §520.8(a).
51. *In re* Marsching, 161 Conn 166, 286 A.2d 306 (1971); Harty v. Board of Bar Examiners, 81 N.M. 116, 464 P.2d 406 (1970); *in re* Church, 111 R.I. 425, 303 A.2d 758 (1973).
52. *In re* Shaikh, 39 N.Y.2d 676, 350 N.E.2d 902, 385 N.Y.S.2d 514 (1976).
53. *In re* St. Amour, 449 P.2d 673 (Alas. 1969); *in re* Stephenson, 511 P.2d 136 (Alas. 1973). *See also supra* note 42.
54. Brown v. Supreme Court of Va., 359 F. Supp. 549 (E.D. Va. 1973), *aff'd*, 414 U.S. 1034 (1973).
55. Hawkins v. Moss, 503 F.2d 1171 (4th Cir. 1974), *cert. denied*, 420 U.S. 928 (1975); *in re* Avery's Petition, 44 Hawaii 597, 358 P.2d 709 (1961).
56. *In re* Reid, 76 Nev. 76, 349 P.2d 446 (1960).
57. Rules of the New York State Court of Appeals, §520.7.

II

Admission *pro haec vice*

What does it mean to allow an attorney to appear *pro haec vice*?

It means that the attorney will be admitted to appear only for the particular case before the court. The literal translation is "for this turn." It is a way of allowing an attorney who is not admitted to the bar of the particular court to participate in a trial or a hearing, if the court is satisfied of the attorney's competence, without requiring the attorney to apply for formal admission.

Does an attorney who is admitted to the bar of a particular state have the right to be admitted *pro haec vice* to another court?

There is no absolute right, but there are certain qualified rights, at least in federal courts. For example, in one recent case, a federal appellate court ordered a federal trial judge to admit an out-of-state lawyer for purposes of defending a tax-evasion case. The court said,

> Admission to a state bar creates a presumption of good moral character that cannot be overcome

merely by the whims of the District Court. An applicant for admission *pro haec vice* who is a member in good standing of a state bar may not be denied the privilege to appear except "on a showing that in any legal matter, whether before the particular district court or in another jurisdiction, he has been guilty of unethical conduct of such a nature as to justify disbarment of a lawyer admitted generally to the bar of the court."

The appellate court ruled that if the trial judge believed there was evidence justifying denial of admission, he was required to

set a hearing date and give the attorney adequate notice of all incidents of alleged misbehavior or unethical behavior that will be charged against him. Specific allegations must be made; general accusations about an attorney's demeanor are insufficient. The hearing must be on the record and present the attorney with adequate opportunity to defend himself and his professional reputation.[1]

These cases deal with federal courts. Are there similar limitations on state courts?

Yes. Where a state recognizes *pro haec vice* admission, its courts do not have absolute power to deny or grant it. In one case, a federal appellate court ruled that a state trial judge's prerogative to exclude out-of-state counsel was "not an absolute right." But in the case before it, the appellate court held that the state judge had not acted unconstitutionally. The state judge denied an out-of-state lawyer's application on the ground that he had "affirmatively refused to limit his out-of-court statements about the case during its pendency." The state appellate courts held that the trial judge had acted properly and the federal appellate court agreed. The out-of-state lawyer in this case was William Kuntsler. The United States Supreme Court denied review.[2]

Do any states have written rules with regard to admissions *pro haec vice*?

Yes. For example, the New York Court of Appeals has issued three rules on this subject. The first simply says that any court of record may allow an attorney or counselor-at-law "or the equivalent from another State, territory, district, or foreign country" to participate "in the trial or argument of any particular cause in which he may be for the time being employed." A second rule allows "an attorney and counselor-at-law" from another jurisdiction to practice in New York while he or she is a graduate student or a graduate assistant, or is employed as a law-school teacher in a "criminal law or poverty law and litigation program in an approved law school in New York State." But the representation must be without fee, and there are certain other requirements. Finally, a graduate of an approved law school who is an "attorney and counselor-at-law" in another jurisdiction may represent clients during his or her employment by a legal-service program. There is an eighteen-month limit on admission under this rule. Again, the representation must be without fee, and other restrictions apply.[3]

Does a state court have to recognize admission *pro haec vice*?

A state can dispense with *pro haec vice* admissions entirely, with some exceptions. The state's legislature or judiciary can, if it wishes, require that every attorney who appears before its courts have passed its state bar examination.[4] The only limitations on this rule are where a federal claim is raised in state court or, in some states, in criminal cases.

How do these limitations apply?

In one case, a corporation involved in antitrust litigation in a federal court in New York retained a California lawyer who was an expert in the area. The lawyer worked for five years, sometimes appearing in the New York federal court. Eventually, the lawyer and the corporation had a dispute about the lawyer's fee and the corporation refused to pay it. The lawyer sued. The corporation contended that payment of the fee would be illegal since the lawyer was practicing in New York without a license (he was admitted in California only). The full Second Circuit, with two judges dissenting, rejected this argument. In the course of its opinion the court said: "[u]nder the privileges and immunities clause of the Constitution, no state can prohibit a citizen with a federal claim or defense from engaging an out-of-state lawyer to collaborate with an in-state lawyer and give legal advice concerning it within the state." The court went on to say:

> In an age of increased specialization and high mobility of the bar, this must comprehend the right to bring to the assistance of an attorney admitted in the resident state a lawyer licensed by "public act" of any other state who is thought best fitted for the task. . . . Indeed, in instances where the federal claim or defense is unpopular, advice and assistance by an out-of-state lawyer may be the only means available for vindication.

But the court limited its ruling to the situation where the out-of-state lawyer is working with local counsel "on a federal claim or defense."[5] Although this case arose in connection with work performed in federal court, its reasoning would apply to work performed in a state court on a federal claim or defense.

Have any state courts ruled that a criminal defendant has a constitutional right to be represented by retained out-of-state counsel if he so chooses?

Perhaps the leading state-court case is from California. A defendant, charged with murder, was represented by a court-appointed California attorney. The defendant and his attorney requested that former United States Attorney General Ramsey Clark be appointed as co-counsel, without fee, to participate in the representation. Mr. Clark was a member of three bars, but not of the California bar. The trial judge refused to appoint him. The California Supreme Court held that this was error and that "the right to appear by retained counsel of one's choice will tolerate the denial of an application for association only in extreme circumstances."[6]

Is there any limitation on a state court's power to withdraw an attorney's admission to practice *pro haec vice* after it has been granted?

Even if a state court is not obligated to admit an out-of-state lawyer to try a case *pro haec vice*, there is some indication that if it does so, it cannot withdraw that admission arbitrarily. In one recent Ohio case, the state court removed an out-of-state lawyer from a case, even though he had earlier been permitted to appear *pro haec vice*. The lawyer received no hearing and had no opportunity to challenge the state judge's reversal. A federal district judge ruled that this was constitutional error. Once the lawyer's "interest" had been initially recognized by the *pro haec vice* admission, that "interest" could not be withdrawn without due-process safeguards. The federal judge enjoined continuation of the state criminal trial until the out-of-state lawyer was given a chance to be heard at a procedurally proper hearing.[7]

If an attorney is admitted *pro haec vice* for a particular proceeding that ends in a mistrial, must a second admission *pro haec vice* be secured for the retrial?

Yes. Admission for the trial does not include admission for the retrial of the matter.[8]

Have any courts ruled that a litigant has an absolute right to be represented by an out-of-state counsel who is not associated with local counsel?

Yes. Relying on the Sixth Amendment's guarantee of the "effective assistance of counsel," at least one federal appellate court has ruled that a defendant in a federal *criminal* case has the absolute right to be represented by an out-of-state attorney admitted in good standing to the courts of another state.[9]

What kind of conduct might justify a court in denying an out-of-state lawyer the right to appear *pro haec vice*?

In one case, California lawyer Melvin Belli was admitted to the United States District Court for the District of Columbia, *pro haec vice*, to try a negligence case arising out of the alleged malpractice of a hospital. The jury returned a sizable verdict, but the trial judge ordered a new trial after concluding that the defendant hospital had been prejudiced because Mr. Belli had improperly informed the jury that the hospital was insured. Before the retrial, the attorney appeared on a nationwide television show and made derogatory remarks about the trial judge and the court. He said, for example, that the trial judge's son represented "all of the hospitals in the District," and he also said that there had been a time, as recently as ten years earlier, when black and white jurors could not sit "on the same side of the courtroom" in the District court. Both these statements, and apparently others, were untrue. On retrial, with the case assigned to a different district judge, Belli's application to appear *pro haec vice* was denied. The judge wrote: "Mr. Belli acted in complete disregard as to the factual accuracy of his statements. Such conduct requires that this Court refuse to admit him to practice in this case."[10]

Obviously, there are many things a lawyer can do to get herself in trouble with the court. In one recent case, attorney F. Lee Bailey was prohibited from appearing in courts of the state of New Jersey after he was found to have violated the Canons of Professional Ethics relating to newspaper publicity. In another case, the fact that an out-of-state lawyer had been found in contempt of court on three prior occasions justified a trial judge's refusal to admit him *pro haec vice*.[11]

Does an indigent defendant in a criminal case, who is entitled to have defense counsel appointed and paid by the state, have a right to have the court appoint an out-of-state counsel?

No. This is true even if the out-of-state counsel is willing to represent the defendant. The state court judge may appoint the out-of-state counsel, but he does not have to.[12] But this rule only applies to counsel appointed by the state.

What if a lawyer admitted in one state renders legal services in another state, other than before a court?

Two things can happen. Conceivably, he can be found guilty of practicing law without a license, but this is not likely. More likely, his clients may refuse to pay him on the ground that he was not legally authorized to render legal advice or service to them. This will be a complete defense unless the attorney can show that the service done in the second state was related to and incidental to legal advice and services the attorney was already providing in the state in which he was admitted.[13]

NOTES

1. *In re* Evans, 524 F.2d 1004, 1007, 1008 (5th Cir. 1975). *See also* Sanders v. Russell, 401 F.2d 241 (5th Cir. 1968); Munoz v. United States District Court, 446 F.2d 434 (9th Cir. 1971); Thomas v. Cassidy, 249 F.2d 91 (4th Cir. 1957), *cert. denied*, 355 U.S. 958 (1958) (granting the district judge discretion to disallow admission).
2. Ross v. Reda, 510 F.2d 1172 (6th Cir. 1975), *cert. denied*, 423 U.S. 892 (1975). For the Ohio state court decisions on this case, *see* State v. Ross, 36 Ohio App. 2d 185, 304 N.E.2d 396 (1973), *appeal dismissed*, 415 U.S. 904 (1974).
3. Rules of the New York State Court of Appeals, §520.8(d).
4. Brown v. Supreme Court of Va., 359 F. Supp. 549 (E.D. Va. 1973), *aff'd.*, 414 U.S. 1034 (1973).
5. Spanos v. Skouras Theatres Corp., 364 F.2d 161, 170 (2d Cir. 1966), *cert. denied*, 385 U.S. 987 (1966). *See also in re* Rappaport, 558 F.2d 87 (2d Cir. 1977).
6. Magee v. Superior Court of City and County of San Francisco, 8 Cal.3d 949, 506 P.2d 1023, 106 Cal. Rptr. 647 (1973).
7. Flynt v. Leis, 434 F. Supp. 481 (S.D. Ohio 1977), *aff'd.*, 574 F.2d 874 (6th Cir. 1978).
8. *In re* Rappaport, *supra* note 5.
9. United States v. Bergamo, 154 F.2d 31 (3d Cir. 1946). *See also* United States v. Bradford, 238 F.2d 395 (2d Cir. 1956), *cert. denied*, 352 U.S. 1002 (1957) (holding that a trial judge "would seem . . . at least in a criminal case" to be required to permit out-of-state counsel to proceed, despite the fact that he had not been admitted in the District, "in the absence of some showing that he lacked the qualifications necessary for the performance of his duties as defense counsel").
10. *In re* Belli, 371 F. Supp. 111 (D.D.C. 1974).

THE RIGHTS OF LAWYERS AND CLIENTS

11. *In re* Bailey, 57 N.J. 451, 273 A.2d 563 (1971); Smith v. Brock, 532 P.2d 843 (Okla. 1975). *See also in re* Rappaport, *supra* note 5 (lawyer properly denied admission *pro haec vice* where he had earlier been suspended in his own state and where he would have to be witness at the trial of the case).
12. Bedrosian v. Mintz, 518 F.2d 396, 401 (2d Cir. 1975).
13. Lozoff v. Shore Heights, Ltd., 66 Ill.2d 398, 362 N.E.2d 1047 (1977); Spivak v. Sachs, 16 N.Y.2d 163, 211 N.E.2d 329, 263 N.Y.S.2d 953 (1965); Appell v. Reiner, 43 N.J. 313, 204 A.2d 146 (1964).

III

Lawyer Discipline

How does a disciplinary proceeding get started?
In a number of ways. A client may complain to a bar association's grievance committee about the conduct of her attorney. An opposing lawyer may make such a complaint. The grievance committee may begin an investigation on its own. Or the court may request that a grievance committee or other appropriate bar association investigative body look into the conduct of a particular lawyer.

Can an attorney sue a client or anyone else who sends information about her to the grievance committee, if the information turns out to be wrong or not to be a violation of any disciplinary rule?
No. Complaints to a grievance committee are absolutely privileged. This means that if a client or anyone else, including an opposing attorney, complains to a grievance committee about the conduct of a member of the bar, the person complaining cannot be sued because of what he says. It doesn't matter if the information in the complaint turns out to be wrong or if the conduct turns out not to be unethical.[1]

THE RIGHTS OF LAWYERS AND CLIENTS

What kind of conduct can justify disciplining an attorney?

Practically any conduct that most reasonable people will consider wrong. Conviction of a felony will almost always result in disbarment. But discipline is possible for many other acts as well, including, in the language of the New York law, "professional misconduct, malpractice, fraud, deceit, crime or misdemeanor, or any conduct prejudicial to the administration of justice. . . ." This language obviously encompasses a broad range of activity.[2]

But is there any document, other than the penal law, to which a disciplining body can look in deciding whether an attorney has been guilty of "professional misconduct"?

Yes, the American Bar Association has promulgated a Code of Professional Responsibility, a lengthy document consisting of nine "canons" that lawyers are expected to obey. Each canon is followed by the "ethical considerations" giving rise to it and the "disciplinary rules" that flow from it.

What are examples of some of the canons?

Canon 1 provides that "A lawyer should assist in maintaining the integrity and competence of the legal profession." Canon 4 says that "A lawyer should preserve the confidences and secrets of a client." Canon 6 says that "A lawyer should represent the client competently." And Canon 9 says that "A lawyer should avoid even the appearance of professional impropriety."

These canons sound rather vague. How does a lawyer know exactly what he or she is supposed to do or not do?

The canons are followed by more detailed ethical considerations and disciplinary rules, but even these are fairly general. Also, it is doubtful that most lawyers ever read them. It is possible to get a more concrete understanding of what constitutes prohibited conduct by reading a court's disciplinary decisions. In addition, most types of conduct that can result in discipline—such as using a client's money or betraying a client's confidence—should be apparent to reasonably intelligent people, lawyers and laymen.

LAWYER DISCIPLINE

Is it correct, then, that a lawyer cannot be disciplined unless he commits a crime or violates the Code of Professional Responsibility?

No. The courts have a residual, discretionary power to conclude that particular conduct is deserving of discipline even though it might not amount to criminal activity or violate the Code of Professional Responsibility.

Is the Code of Professional Responsibility the same as a state's statute?

Not necessarily. While all states have adopted the Code, sometimes with modifications, its legal force varies from state to state. For example, in New York, although failure to abide by the Code, as adopted by the State Bar, is defined as "misconduct," the Code does not have "the status of decisional or statutory law." Nevertheless, the Court of Appeals has held that "the courts should not denigrate [the Code] by indifference." In other words, the New York courts will look to the Code for guidance in determining whether particular conduct is unethical or improper.[3]

Some states give the Code greater force than New York. For example, the Louisiana Supreme Court recently said:

> The Canons are "statements of axiomatic norms, expressing in general terms the standards of professional conduct expected of lawyers in their relationship with the public, with the legal system, and with the legal profession." . . . Ethical Considerations are "aspirational in character," and they represent "the objectives toward which every member of the profession should strive." The Disciplinary Rules are mandatory in character. They "state the minimal level of conduct below which no lawyer can fall without being subject to disciplinary action."

Maryland also treats the Disciplinary Rules as representing "the mandatory minimum level of conduct required by members of the Bar." The Pennsylvania Supreme Court has also ruled that the Code has "the force of statutory rules of conduct for lawyers."[4]

What punishments are available to a disciplining body if a lawyer engages in illegal or unethical conduct?

Different states have different punishments, or different names for the same punishment. Generally, these fall into the following classifications. The ultimate punishment is disbarment. A disbarred lawyer is no longer a lawyer. Next is suspension from the practice of law. Suspension can last anywhere from a few days up to three or more years, depending on the jurisdiction. In some jurisdictions, an attorney suspended for a definite period of time is nevertheless not automatically entitled to readmission when that time expires, but must reapply for admission and demonstrate his good moral character. In addition to disbarment and suspension, an attorney may also be publicly censured for unethical or illegal conduct. Many states also have provisions under which an attorney can be formally reprimanded by the ethics or grievance committee of a bar association. Finally, in a number of states an investigation can end with a simple letter of admonition from a bar-association official. Of course, we have been discussing the remedies available to disciplinary bodies. If a lawyer does something illegal, he can also be criminally prosecuted.

Are disciplinary proceedings confidential?

Generally yes, at least until a court concludes that there has been misconduct and determines the punishment.

But what if the matter never gets to court, if it is resolved by an informal letter of admonition or a formal reprimand?

Then it will generally remain confidential. Some states, however, have opted for more open disciplinary proceedings. In these states, for example Michigan and Georgia, once a finding of probable cause to believe that an attorney is guilty of a disciplinary violation has been made, the hearing to determine the accuracy of that charge is generally open to the public. Florida provides for waiver of confidentiality where the attorney has committed a felony or has engaged in conduct which constitutes a general unfitness to practice law, or when public interest clearly demands it. California provides for discretionary public reproval of attorneys through publication in the state bar journal. Vermont does not require confidentiality where the investigation of attorney misconduct is predicated upon a criminal conviction. Confidentiality also ends in Vermont once the state disciplinary body prefers charges.[5]

Is confidentiality a good thing?

A balance must be struck between protecting an attorney charged with a disciplinary violation, where the charges have not yet been proved, and protecting the public against incompetent or dishonest lawyers. Confidentiality has been the rule in most states for a long time. But now, some experts are beginning to believe that this rule has resulted in a loss of public confidence in the ability of the bar to police itself. Recently, the Association of the Bar of the City of New York, in a report on its grievance system by a Committee on Grievance Procedures, recommended that the confidentiality rule be limited and that formal hearings on attorney misconduct be open to the public.[6]

Who decides whether the alleged misconduct should be handled with a simple admonition or reprimand, on the one hand, or should result in a court proceeding leading to censure, suspension, or disbarment?

This is usually a decision for the bar association grievance committee or the particular body charged with overseeing the conduct of attorneys in the state.

But aren't these committees or bodies simply composed of other lawyers?

Generally, yes. This has also resulted in a failure of public confidence in the grievance mechanism. Some states have begun to appoint lay people to grievance committees—for example, Colorado, Georgia, Michigan, Minnesota, Washington, and Wisconsin.[7]

Which branch of government has authority to determine the grounds and methods of discipline?

Although state legislatures may pass laws generally outlining procedure, which the courts will recognize, the actual power belongs to the courts. Consider the following quotes—the first is from a federal court of appeals, ruling in a lawsuit by an applicant to the Arkansas bar; the second is from the Iowa Supreme Court:

> The principle is firmly established that the judicial branch of the government, acting through the courts, has exclusive jurisdiction to admit, control, and disbar attorneys. The courts may and frequently do honor implementing legislation, but clearly are not bound so to do.[8]

> We claim the inherent constitutional power to license lawyers and acknowledge the duty to censure, suspend, or revoke licenses to practice when a lawyer has committed an offense which involves deceit, is prejudicial to the administration of justice, and adversely reflects on such a person's fitness as a member of the bar.[9]

Can a disbarred attorney be readmitted?

Sometimes. It depends upon the reason for disbarment. Different states apply different rules. Florida seems to be the most lenient state.[10] In fact, even an attorney who has been suspended or disbarred in another jurisdiction is not automatically disqualified for admission to the Florida bar exam.[11] Generally, an attorney will have a strict burden of proof before she will be readmitted after disbarment.[12] Even a lawyer who has only been suspended may, in some states, be required to show that she has been rehabilitated before she can be readmitted.[13] The primary question in an application for readmission is the attorney's present moral fitness.[14] Recently, the Maryland Court of Appeals ruled that the factors to be considered in evaluating a petition for reinstatement to the bar are:

1. the nature and circumstances of the original misconduct;
2. petitioner's subsequent conduct and reformation;
3. his present character;
4. his present qualifications and competence to practice law.[15]

New York also recognizes reinstatement under certain conditions.[16]

How about a lawyer who is disbarred after conviction for a felony?

Some states would not allow a convicted felon to reapply for admission.[17] On the other hand, other states have readmitted convicted felons.[18]

What if a lawyer is disbarred because he has been convicted of a crime and his conviction is then reversed?

The lawyer must be readmitted promptly. In some states, the readmission is automatic and retroactive.[19] In some other states, readmission can be delayed pending an immediate investigation by an appropriate bar association grievance committee to see whether it will bring charges against the lawyer based on the same factual allegations that led to the criminal charges.[20] But if the bar association does not act quickly, the lawyer will be entitled to readmission.[21]

Does this mean that a lawyer who is acquitted on a criminal charge or whose conviction is later reversed and thrown out can nevertheless be the subject of a disciplinary proceeding?

Absolutely. One has nothing to do with the other. Even though the facts of the criminal trial did not prove a crime, or that the lawyer had committed a crime, the very same facts may justify a disciplinary sanction. This is because the goals of the criminal trial and the goals of the disciplinary proceeding differ. The purpose of a disciplinary proceeding is to protect the integrity of the judicial system and the public against an incompetent or dishonest lawyer.[22]

But doesn't that mean that the lawyer is placed in double jeopardy?

Not at all. The lawyer is not being tried for the same crime twice. Since the two proceedings have different objectives, the lawyer is not placed in double jeopardy. This is true even though a disciplinary proceeding is recognized to be "quasi-criminal."[23]

If a conviction is reversed for a new trial, is the lawyer entitled to be readmitted even before the new trial begins?

Yes, unless the bar association's grievance committee or other appropriate prosecuting body proceeds against her promptly. The fact that the lawyer is *charged* with a crime does not justify preventing her from practicing her profession.[24]

What if a lawyer is convicted of a crime and then pardoned?

This will not automatically entitle him to readmission. A certificate relieving a convicted felon from the disabilities that generally accompany conviction carries even less weight in an application for readmission.[25]

What are some examples of conduct warranting discipline?

In one case an attorney forged the name of a special referee to a report and then forged the name of the judge. He was disbarred.[26] In another case, an attorney knowingly entered into a bigamous marriage with his client without telling the client that she was not free to marry. The attorney later divorced the client while hiding from the court the fact that the client was pregnant. He was suspended from practice for one year.[27] In another case, an attorney secured divorces between parties who he knew were not bona fide residents of the state, although he represented to the court that they were. He was disbarred.[28]

A judge who had *ex parte* communications with one party to a lawsuit was disbarred.[29] In one case, the court, though only suspending the lawyer, held that grossly negligent disregard of a client's interests could lead to disbarment even without willfulness.[30] In another case, an attorney convinced his long-time friend and neighbor, who was unsophisticated in business affairs, to convey certain real property to the attorney's relative for about one-fifth of its value. The agreement provided that the neighbor could repurchase the property at the end of one year unless the property had been taken in eminent-domain proceedings. The attorney was aware that such proceedings were likely and did not advise the neighbor. This was held a disciplinary violation and the attorney received a three-month suspension.[31] Finally, in one case an attorney refused to refund to a client money that belonged to the client and which the attorney had withdrawn from his escrow account without the client's consent. He was disbarred.[32]

The range of punishment seems very broad. How do the courts assure consistency?

While it is true that each court is aware of other cases that have come before it and of the actions of other courts in the state with the power to discipline, the decisions in disciplinary cases so depend on the particular facts and the court's perception of the true character of the attorney, that it is practically impossible to find consistency in the decisions. In fact, when we compare results between states, rather than simply within the same state, the differences in attitude toward attorney misconduct sometimes seem extreme.

What are some examples?

Not long ago, two cases were decided by a New York State appeals court on the same day. In one, a young lawyer, who had been admitted to the bar for only seven years, had been convicted of a misdemeanor—offering a false document for filing. He received a $1,000 fine and probation. The false document was an application to the State Liquor Authority, in which the lawyer stated that the company for which he was seeking a wholesale beer license was owned solely by himself and a cousin. In fact, there were three silent partners. The attorney was suspended for two years. In the other case, a lawyer, who had been a member of the bar for fifty years, had been convicted in federal court of conspiracy to violate federal security laws and fraud in the purchase and sale of securities, a felony. He received a $5,000 fine. The same court that suspended the first attorney for two years concluded that the punishment in the second case should be only a censure.[33]

In another case, an attorney was found guilty in federal court of certain felonies relating to securities. He received a four-month sentence and twenty months of probation. The court noted that the attorney had "an otherwise unblemished record" and that he was held in high regard "by many people with distinguished public service. He is a graduate of an eminent law school, served in the Judge Advocate Corps of the United States Army . . . and was at one time law secretary" to a federal judge. He was suspended for two years.[34]

In another case, a lawyer failed to prosecute a client's negligence claim within the time required by the statute of limitations. He then made false statements to the representative of the grievance committee about what had really happened. The attorney paid the client $2,000 to cover the client's loss. He was suspended for three months.[35]

An attorney who had personally used funds in his escrow account which belonged to a client, but made immediate restitution after a complaint had been filed with the grievance committee, was suspended for three months.[36] The same penalty was given to an attorney who "falsely advised his client that the case was in arbitration, fabricated documentary evidence which he exhibited to his client to support this false assertion and, upon the client's discovery of the misrepresentation, refused to respond to inquiries by the client's new counsel."[37]

Another attorney was suspended from practice for three years after he was convicted in federal court of attempting to bribe a police officer to give false testimony at a criminal trial. The attorney spent thirteen months in jail and was fined $10,000.[38]

Can an attorney appeal his punishment or finding of unethical conduct?

The only "review" usually open to an attorney who is suspended or disbarred by the highest state court charged with that responsibility is to apply for readmission and prove to the court that he is now capable of practicing law. See next question and the next chapter (at notes 22-25 and 29-30).

What recourse does an attorney who is the subject of disciplinary proceeding have to the federal courts?

Not much. Although, as we shall see, constitutional requirements must be observed at disciplinary proceedings, and although it is possible, in some extreme cases, for a federal court to interfere in an ongoing proceeding, a federal forum is rarely available to the attorney, either during or after the proceeding.

There is one exception to this. A lawyer who has been disciplined and who believes that the discipline has violated his federal constitutional rights, can seek *direct* review of the state decision in the United States Supreme Court.[89] But he will generally not be able to challenge the state proceeding collaterally by bringing an action in the federal district court while the state proceedings are in progress.[40]

In order to be disciplined, must the lawyer's misconduct relate to something she has done or failed to do in her professional capacity?

No. The clearest example of this is if a lawyer commits a crime entirely unrelated to the practice of law. She may nevertheless be disciplined and even disbarred, if the criminal activity is serious enough. In some states, like New York, conviction of a felony requires automatic disbarment regardless of the felony, without a hearing.

But some of the examples given before involve New York lawyers who were convicted of felonies in federal court; yet they were not automatically disbarred. How come?

In New York until recently, conviction of a federal felony did not lead to automatic disbarment if the same crime under the state's own penal law would only be a misdemeanor. This situation arises most frequently when an attorney is convicted in federal court of tax evasion or other tax-related offenses. The offense may be a federal felony, but is considered a misdemeanor under the analogous New York statute. So in one case, where an attorney entered a guilty plea to having filed a false and fraudulent income tax return, he was only censured.[41] In another case, an attorney was convicted in federal court of conspiring to illegally melt silver coins of the United States. He too was censured.[42] In each of these cases, the court was able to give reduced punishments because the attorney was not convicted of a felony in the state of New York. If he had been, the court would have had no discretion. The attorney would be automatically disbarred.

Why was this the rule in New York "until recently"?

In 1940, the New York Court of Appeals ruled that the law requiring automatic disbarment on conviction of a felony did not apply where the conviction occurred in a federal court unless the federal felony was also a felony under New York law. But if the federal felony was a misdemeanor under New York law, disbarment would not be automatic. Rather, there would be a hearing into the underlying acts and the appropriate punishment, including possible disbarment, determined.[43]

After this decision, there were many efforts to determine whether a particular federal felony was or was not a felony under New York law. Since federal and state criminal statutes are not mirror images of each other, this was not always easy to do. Surely the most important area was tax crimes, since a tax violation that was a felony under federal law would often be a state misdemeanor.

Recently, the New York Court of Appeals considered the case of a lawyer who had been convicted in federal court of filing false and fraudulent documents with the Immigration and Naturalization Service. This was a federal felony. The lower state court concluded that the particular federal statute involved "was not a mirror equivalent of the New York State crime" dealing with the same subject matter. It therefore refused to automatically disbar the lawyer, but ordered a hearing. The highest state court reversed.[44] Four of the seven judges at first seemed to say that conviction of any federal felony would result in New York State disbarment, regardless of the relative seriousness with which the state considered the particular crime. "We now perceive little or no reason for distinguishing between conviction of a federal felony and conviction of a New York State felony as a predicate for professional discipline," said the majority. But then the majority added a qualifier: "Certainly is this so, when, as here, there is a New York State felony of substantially the same elements." It did not matter that the parallel between the state and federal laws was not exact.

Since the majority decision did not fully indicate

whether conviction of a federal felony will always result in automatic disbarment, three other judges, concurring, wrote a separate opinion expressing their understanding that the majority opinion "did not intend to imply that all felony convictions in federal courts would necessarily dictate the same result" as a felony conviction in state court. The concurring judges felt that there might be certain felony convictions in federal court which "should not be considered of sufficient gravity to automatically rebut the presumption of integrity underlying an attorney's license to practice law in this State." As an example, the concurring judges mentioned convictions for obscenity, where local community standards are critical.

The court has again addressed the issue and, this time, the same four judge majority ruled that the automatic disbarment rule should apply to any federal felony, whatever its equivalent in New York law. Lower courts have applied the rule retroactively and to the most frequent federal felony, failure to file taxes.[45]

What are other examples of conduct for which an attorney can be disciplined and which do not arise out of the practice of his profession?

In one case, an attorney was disciplined for acts committed before he was admitted to the bar, but not discovered until later. The conduct involved making false representations in order to obtain more money than the attorney was due.[46] Violation of a fiduciary relationship can also lead to discipline.[47] Engaging in fraudulent conduct as a stockholder and officer of a corporation can warrant discipline.[48] It has even been held that a lawyer who enters business, while remaining a member of the bar, must conduct himself in the business according to the standards imposed on members of the bar, even if the standards in the business community are lower.[49] Finally, an attorney was found subject to discipline for deceitful activities in which he engaged in order to aid the reelection of a candidate for President of the United States.[50]

Can an attorney who is holding office be disciplined for conduct he undertakes in his political capacity even though he is not acting in his capacity as an attorney?

Yes. Richard Nixon was disbarred by the New York courts for improper use of his powers while President of the United States,[51] although, even here, the court stressed that the "gravamen" of his conduct was "obstruction of the due administration of justice," which is also a crime.

Income-tax violations seem to be treated with greater leniency than other crimes. Is this always true?

Some states do seem to distinguish, at least unofficially, between convictions for income-tax violations and other kinds of convictions, even though both may involve fraud for personal gain. In some states, however, the willful attempt to evade the payment of income taxes is treated more harshly. The Maryland Supreme Court recently held, in a disciplinary proceeding involving former Vice-President Spiro T. Agnew, that "when a member of the bar is shown to be willfully dishonest for personal gain by means of fraud, deceit, cheating, or like conduct, absent the most compelling extenuating circumstances, not shown to be present here, disbarment [follows] as a matter of course." Agnew, it will be remembered, pleaded no contest to a charge that he willfully attempted to evade the payment of federal taxes.[52]

But Agnew pleaded "no contest" or "nolo contendere." Is this the same as being convicted?

Yes. A no-contest plea supports a judgment of conviction of a crime and is a valid basis for disciplinary action. The plea simply means that the defendant will not contest or try to defend against the charge.[53]

If an attorney is convicted of a crime and a disciplinary proceeding is then commenced against him, can he relitigate the facts of the criminal case in the disciplinary proceeding?

No. The issue of guilt may not be relitigated. Since the standard of proof required to convict a person of a crime is higher than the standard required to establish an ethical violation, the facts necessarily found at the criminal trial are conclusive on the attorney at the disciplinary hearing. The attorney may, however, introduce evidence to explain or mitigate the significance of his criminal conviction. This will assist the court in determining the appropriate sanction.[54]

Can an attorney be disciplined simply because she was ignorant of the law?

Yes. If the ignorance is so extensive that it amounts to serious professional incompetence, discipline is possible. On the other hand, if there is not shown a general incompetence to practice law, discipline is unlikely. For example, in one California case decided more than thirty years ago, but still often cited, the court held that the prosecuting grievance committee did not have authority to recommend discipline "for lack of legal learning, as a general charge." A lawyer

> must perform his duties to the best of his individual ability, not the standard of ability required of lawyers generally in the community. Mere ignorance of the law in conducting the affairs of his client in good faith is not a cause for discipline. The nearest approach to such conduct is negligence as a ground for discipline when the neglect is so serious as to constitute a violation of his oath as an attorney.[55]

Under this case, even though a lawyer may not be guilty of such ignorance justifying discipline, the same conduct may support a private malpractice action by the client against the attorney, a subject we shall discuss later.

Other courts seem more willing to discipline a lawyer based on his ignorance.[56] Of course, if a lawyer displays a pattern of disregard for the interests of his client, regardless of his good faith, simply because he can't "get it together," the courts will likely act to suspend him simply to protect the public.[57] Some courts call such a pattern of disregard for clients the equivalent of professional incompetence, justifying discipline.[58]

What about cases where an attorney neglects a client's case and keeps putting off the work he is required to do?

This can result in discipline, even disbarment.[59]

THE RIGHTS OF LAWYERS AND CLIENTS

Is it improper for a lawyer to regularly fail to respond to telephone calls and correspondence from other lawyers and clients?

Yes. A consistent failure to respond to telephone calls and correspondence has been held to violate the Code of Professional Responsibility.[60]

Does it ever happen that an attorney is disciplined for charging too much?

Rarely, although there is a disciplinary rule against it. The rule says: "A lawyer shall not enter into an agreement for, charge, or collect an illegal or clearly excessive fee." So a merely excessive fee is acceptable. Only a "clearly excessive" one is not.[61] The cases are very few where an attorney has been disciplined for charging too much.[62]

Is an attorney subject to discipline for the misconduct of her partners?

Generally, yes. The courts will look to see if the attorney knew or should have known about the misconduct. An attorney cannot avoid responsibility by intentionally turning her head the other way.[63] On the other hand, where the partner has acted without the knowledge of the attorney and where the attorney could not have been expected to know about the partner's misconduct, she will not be held responsible.[64]

Can a lawyer who represents one side of a case talk to the clients who are on the other side?

No, unless one of the following exceptions apply. First, if the opposing party is not represented by a lawyer and is not going to retain a lawyer, obviously he will be the only person the opposing lawyer can talk to. Nevertheless, the lawyer has the primary duty of first advising the adversary to secure counsel.[65] Second, the prohibition on communication with an adversary does not apply if the discussion is about a subject other than the subject of the representation.[66] Third, a lawyer can speak to an adversary lawyer's client if the adversary lawyer consents.[67] Finally, if the party on the other side is a corporation, there is some authority that the opposing lawyer can speak to at least low-level employees or agents of the corporation.[68] But there is also authority that he may not speak to any employee or agent of the corporation if the corporation is represented by counsel.[69]

Are prosecutors or district attorneys ever disciplined?
Rarely, but it does happen. In one case, a prosecutor was reprimanded after refusing to plea-bargain with certain criminal defendants on the same basis as he had previously bargained with another defendant. The prosecutor's reason was his dislike of the attorneys representing the defendants. The court held that this conduct served to harass or maliciously injure another and was prejudicial to the administration of criminal justice.[70]

If a prosecutor violates a disciplinary provision or otherwise acts improperly, can a criminal defendant sue him for damages in addition to referring the case to the grievance committee?
Rarely. Although the prosecutor will be subject to disciplinary procedures for his conduct, the Supreme Court has ruled that a prosecutor who acts improperly in connection with his prosecutorial responsibilities nevertheless has absolute immunity from suit for any harm arising out of his improper action.[71] On the other hand, even this case seemed to leave a loophole. If a prosecutor's misconduct arises not out of his prosecutorial duties, but in his role as administrator or investigative officer, there may not be absolute immunity. Instead, in these situations, the prosecutor may be liable for misconduct carried out in bad faith or intentionally. At least one court has held that this exception to absolute immunity does apply.[72]

Is it improper for a lawyer to copy the forms used by another lawyer word for word?
No. Legal forms are not copyrightable. If another lawyer has been able to come up with clever and acceptable ways of preparing legal papers, they can be copied word for word without impropriety.[73]

Is it a defense to a disciplinary proceeding that the attorney was under great mental or emotional strain at the time the offending conduct took place?

No. Mental and emotional strain, and psychiatric testimony showing it, may be admissible to explain the misconduct as an aid in determining the proper sanction, but it will not be allowed to justify the misconduct or exonerate the attorney from his responsibility.[74]

What are the defenses to a charge of misconduct?

Practically the only defense that will succeed is that the misconduct never occurred. Most other defenses which might spring to mind have been rejected. For example, if an attorney commingles funds belonging to a client with his own funds, he is guilty of an ethical violation and "neither good faith nor restitution" will be a defense.[75] The fact that nobody may have been injured by the attorney's misconduct is not a defense.[76] The fact that commingling of funds might occur through mismanagement is not a defense.[77] The fact that the client may have suffered no monetary loss as a result of the attorney's misconduct does not preclude discipline.[78] Failure of the aggrieved client to complain about the misconduct, or even her acquiescence in it, is not a defense.[79] Ignorance of the Code of Professional Responsibility is no defense.[80] Absence of any intention to gain personally as a result of the misconduct is no defense.[81] The fact that the conduct which serves as the basis of the charge occurred many years ago is no defense, since there is no statute of limitations on violations of the Code of Professional Responsibility.[82] The fact that the violative conduct occurred at the client's direction is no defense.[83]

What if an attorney, charged with taking a client's money, repays the client and has the client sign a release? Will this be a defense to a disciplinary proceeding?

No. It might be relevant to the consideration of the appropriate penalty, but it is not a defense to discipline.[84]

What if an attorney is acquitted on a criminal charge? Can he still be disciplined for the same conduct?

Yes. As we have said, the two proceedings have nothing to do with each other.[85]

Can an attorney be disciplined if she becomes mentally or emotionally incapable of practicing law?

Yes. Since discipline is not simply intended as punishment, but as a means to protect the public from persons not capable, for any reason, of practicing law, mental or emotional instability can serve as the basis for suspension or even disbarment.[86]

How do the disciplinary bodies learn about mental or emotional incompetence?

Often some other professional failure will come to the attention of the grievance body, and in the course of its investigation, the attorney's mental or emotional state will become apparent.[87] In addition, an attorney may be judged mentally incompetent in connection with a separate court proceeding.[88] Or an attorney might be judged incompetent to proceed to trial in a criminal proceeding against him.[89]

If an attorney is suspended because of mental illness, can he reapply for admission?

Yes. Such a suspension should only be for the period of the mental or emotional instability. It should be without prejudice to a reapplication for admission to the bar "at such time as he can prove that he is competent to resume the practice of law."[90]

What happens to the attorney's practice when she is suspended for reasons of mental incompetence?

The court will appoint other attorneys to examine the suspended lawyer's files and take any action needed to protect the interests of clients.[91]

Can an attorney be required to submit to a physical and mental examination?

Yes. There must be some evidence showing that such a requirement is appropriate, but if it is, the attorney can be required to submit to examination. In one case, the lawyer was given the choice of any doctor on a list maintained by the court. The lawyer also had the right to have his own physician present at the examination.[92]

Will an attorney's (or a bar applicant's) purely private lifestyle ever serve as a basis for discipline (or exclusion from the bar)?

There was a time when a lawyer's purely private lifestyle could serve as the basis for discipline. For example, in one old case a divorced attorney was disbarred on the ground of his immoral conduct because he had sexual relations with an unmarried, mentally deficient dwarf, who became pregnant.[93] In another more recent case, an attorney was disbarred on evidence showing that he kept and maintained a disorderly house, and knew that the premises were used for immoral purposes.[94] Seduction under promise of marriage was at one time held a ground for disbarment.[95] A case from 1895, however, held that it did not constitute misconduct warranting discipline that an attorney seduced his young secretary.[96]

Today, with certain notable exceptions, one rarely finds situations in which an attorney is disciplined or an applicant is denied admission to the bar because of purely private conduct. The Oregon Supreme Court made an important distinction in a recent case involving a lawyer who was being disciplined for repeatedly appearing in court intoxicated.

> The personal conduct of an attorney, including the use of intoxicating liquor, may not be a ground for disciplinary action, even when below acceptable social standards. But an attorney's appearance in court in an intoxicated condition to represent a client is now generally held to be a ground for disciplinary action against him, at least when such conduct is repeated over a substantial period of time and after warnings of the possible consequences. . . .

In that case, the attorney was suspended from practice for one year.[97]

Occasionally, even in more recent times, there are cases where a lawyer's sexual interests spill over into an area that reflects on his ability to practice law. In a 1957 New York case, a lawyer was found to have

> lured young women to his premises by advertisements for help wanted, sought to illicit from them answers to highly improper questions by giving assurances that as a lawyer he would keep such answers in strict confidence, . . . made indecent proposals, and attempted assault with intent to commit rape.

It was also found that the lawyer was insane at the time he engaged in this conduct. He was disbarred.[98]

What are the "notable exceptions" to the trend away from considering a lawyer's purely private life?

According to the July, 1978 A.B.A. Journal, a young lawyer was found morally unfit because she was living with a man not her husband. The case is on appeal. Or consider Harris Kimball. Mr. Kimball was admitted to the Florida bar in 1953. He was disbarred in 1957 after an inquiry concluded that he committed an act "contrary to good morals and in violation of the laws of the State." The "act" involved the commission of consensual homosexual sodomy on a public beach at night. Some fifteen years later, Kimball applied for admission to the bar of the state of New York. The Committee on Character and Fitness recommended him "notwithstanding the admission of the applicant to being a homosexual and having engaged in homosexual acts." The intermediate appellate state court nevertheless denied the application for admission by a vote of three to two.[99] On appeal, the Court of Appeals ruled that although Kimball's "status and past conduct may be now and has been in the past violative of accepted norms, they are not controlling, albeit relevant, in assessing character bearing on the right to practice law in this State." The Court of Appeals rejected the argument that the Florida disbarment should disqualify Kimball from membership in the New York bar.[100]

Even the Florida courts have become somewhat more enlightened recently. An applicant to its bar, who admitted he was homosexual, was allowed to qualify. The Supreme

Court of Florida noted that the applicant had not been asked if he had ever actually engaged in homosexual conduct.[101]

NOTES

1. Wiener v. Weintraub, 22 N.Y.2d 330, 239 N.E.2d 540, 292 N.Y.S.2d 667 (1968); Bein v. Lewis, 47 App.Div.2d 538, 363 N.Y.S.2d 116 (2d Dept. 1975); Franklin v. Blank, 86 N.M. 585, 525 P.2d 945 (1974); Kerpelman v. Bricker, 23 Md. App. 628, 329 A.2d 423 (Ct. of Sp. App. 1974); Ramstead v. Morgan, 219 Or. 383, 347 P.2d 594 (1959); McCurdy v. Hughes, 63 N.D. 435, 248 N.W. 512 (1933).
2. N.Y. JUD. LAW §90(2) (McKinney).
3. *In re* Estate of Weinstock, 40 N.Y.2d 1, 351 N.E.2d 647, 386 N.Y.S.2d 1 (1976).
4. Louisiana State Bar Ass'n v. Edwins, —— La. ——, 329 So. 2d 437 (1976); Andresen v. Bar Ass'n of Montgomery County, 269 Md. 313, 305 A.2d 845 (1973); Slater v. Rimar, Inc., 462 Pa. 138, 338 A.2d 584 (1975).
5. Association of the Bar of the City of New York, REPORT on the GRIEVANCE SYSTEM (1976) at p. 18.
6. *Ibid.*, p. 23.
7. Rule 242, Rules of the Supreme Court of Colorado for Discipline of Attorneys; Rule 4-201, Rules and Regulations for Organization and Government of the State Bar of Georgia; Rule 16, Supreme Court Rules Concerning the State Bar of Michigan; Rule III, Rules on Professional Responsibility Governing Members of the Minnesota Bar; Rule 2.4(g), Rules for Discipline of Attorneys, the Supreme Court of the State of Washington; Section 256.281(1), Wisconsin Supreme Court Disciplinary Rules.
8. Feldman v. State Bd. of Law Examiners, 438 F.2d 699, 702 (8th Cir. 1971).
9. Committee on Professional Ethics and Conduct v. Toomey, —— Iowa, ——, 236 N.W. 2d 39, 40 (1975).
10. *In re* Rassner, 265 So.2d 363 (Fla. 1972).
11. *In re* Question of Law Certified to the Supreme Court of Fla. Bd. of Bar Examiners, 265 So.2d 1 (Fla. 1972). *But cf. In re* Florida Board of Bar Examiners, 350 So.2d 1072 (Fla. 1977).

12. Applewhite v. Kentucky State Bar Ass'n., 503 S.W.2d 498 (Ky. 1972).
13. Segretti v. State Bar of Cal., 15 Cal.3d 878, 544 P.2d 929, 126 Cal. Rptr. 793 (1976).
14. Resner v. State Bar of Cal., 67 Cal.2d 799, 433 P.2d 748, 63 Cal. Rptr. 740 (1967).
15. *In re* Barton, 273 Md. 377, 329 A.2d 102 (1974).
16. Rules of the New York State Supreme Court, Appellate Division, First Department, §603.14.
17. People v. Buckles, 167 Colo. 64, 453 P.2d 404 (1968). *Cf.* N.Y. JUD. LAW §90(4) (McKinney) (by implication). *In re* Sugarman, 64 App. Div. 2d 166, 409 N.Y.S.2d 224 (1st Dept. 1978).
18. *In re* Hiss, 368 Mass. 447, 333 N.E.2d 429 (1975).
19. *In re* McDonald, 292 Ala. 426, 296 So.2d 141 (1974).
20. *In re* Barash, 20 N.Y.2d 154, 228 N.E.2d 896, 281 N.Y.S.2d 997 (1967).
21. *In re* Docherty, 42 App. Div. 2d 117, 345 N.Y.S.2d 737 (4th Dept. 1973). *See also in re* Echeles, 374 F.2d 780 (7th Cir. 1967), holding that "minimum standards of fairness" require reinstatement of the suspended attorney after reversal of his conviction, even if the reversal was based on the technicality of improper joinder.
22. *In re* Echeles, 430 F.2d 347 (7th Cir. 1970); Stratmore v. State Bar of Cal., 14 Cal.3d 887, 538 P.2d 229, 123 Cal. Rptr. 101 (1975); *In re* Nesselson, 35 Ill. 2d 454, 220 N.E.2d 409 (1966) (discipline is not imposed primarily to punish, but to protect the public and maintain the reputation and dignity of the legal profession).
23. *In re* Ruffalo, 390 U.S. 544, 551 (1968).
24. *In re* Barash, *supra* note 20.
25. *In re* Beck, 246 Ind. 141, 342 N.E.2d 611 (1976); N.Y. JUD LAW, §90(5) (McKinney); *In re* Harrington, —— Vt. ——, 367 A.2d 161 (1976). *But see in re* Florida Bd. of Bar Examiners, 183 So.2d 688 (Fla. 1966); *in re* Sugarman, 51 App. Div. 2d 170, 380 N.Y.S.2d 12 (1st Dept. 1976) (certificate).
26. State *ex rel.* McLeod v. Belcher, 249 S.C. 301. 153 S.E.2d 921 (1967).
27. Florida Bar v. Smith, 195 So. 2d 852 (Fla. 1967).
28. *In re* Griffith, 283 Ala. 527, 219 So.2d 357 (1969).
29. *In re* Hasler, 447 S.W.2d 65 (Mo. 1969).
30. Demain v. State Bar of Cal., 3 Cal.3d 381, 475 P.2d 652 90 Cal. Rptr. 420 (1970) (dicta).
31. *In re* Hurd, 69 N.J. 316, 354 A.2d 78 (1976).
32. Allgeier v. Johnson, 421 Pa. 342, 219 A.2d 593 (1966).

33. *In re* Goldstein, 49 App. Div. 2d 196, 374 N.Y.S.2d 14 (1st Dept. 1975); *in re* Weisman, 49 App. Div. 2d 180, 374 N.Y.S.2d 311 (1st Dept. 1975).

34. *In re* Persky, 49 App. Div. 2d 353, 374 N.Y.S.2d 665 (1st Dept. 1975).

35. *In re* Cohen, 47 App. Div. 2d 357, 367 N.Y.S.2d 14 (1st Dept. 1975).

36. *In re* Tashker, 45 App. Div. 2d 573, 360 N.Y.S.2d 26 (1st Dept. 1974).

37. *In re* Nicholson, 48 App. Div. 2d 94, 367 N.Y.S.2d 788, 789 (1st Dept. 1975).

38. *In re* Caiola, 48, App. Div. 2d 85, 368 N.Y.S.2d 17 (1st Dept. 1975).

39. Tang v. Appellate Div. of N.Y. Sup. Ct., 487 F.2d 138, 141 (2d Cir. 1973), *cert. denied*, 416 U.S. 906 (1974).

40. *Ibid.*; Turco v. Monroe County Bar Ass'n, 554 F.2d 515 (2d Cir. 1977), *cert. denied*, 434 U.S. 834 (Oct. 3, 1977); Anonymous v. Association of the Bar of the City of N.Y., 515 F.2d 427 (2d Cir. 1975), *cert. denied*, 423 U.S. 863 (1975); Anonymous v. Bar Ass'n of Erie County, 515 F.2d 435 (2d Cir. 1975), *cert. denied*, 423 U.S. 840 (1975). *But cf.* the Supreme Court's affirmance of Mildner v. Gulotta, 405 F. Supp. 182 (E.D.N.Y. 1975), *aff'd*, 425 U.S. 901 (1976), and the treatment of this affirmance for precedential purposes in Turco, *supra*, at 521–22.

41. *In re* Hoffman, 48 App. Div. 2d 81, 368 N.Y.S.2d 19 (1st Dept. 1975). *See also in re* Palmieri, 101 R.I. 775, 226 A.2d 813 (1967).

42. *In re* Robinson, 45 App. Div. 2d 519, 360 N.Y.S.2d 12 (1st Dept. 1974).

43. *In re* Donegan, 282 N.Y. 285, 26 N.E.2d 260 (1940).

44. *In re* Chu, 42 N.Y.2d 490, 398 N.Y.S.2d 1001, 369 N.E. 2d 1 (1977).

45. Joint Bar Assoc. v. Thies, ——N.Y.2d ——, —— N.Y.S. 2d ——, —— N.E.2d —— (Oct. 19, 1978). *In re* Cahn, 59 App. Div. 2d 179, 400 N.Y.S.2d 547 (2d Dept. 1977). Joint Bar Assoc. v. Rosenberg, 62 App. Div. 2d 1065, 406 N.Y.S.2d 492 (2d Dept. 1978).

46. Stratmore, *supra* note 22.

47. Crooks v. State Bar of Cal., 3 Cal.3d 346, 475 P.2d 872, 90 Cal. Rptr. 600 (1970).

48. *In re* Kirtz, 494 S.W.2d 324 (Mo. 1973).

49. *In re* Madera, 39 App. Div. 2d 202, 333 N.Y.S.2d 329 (2d Dept. 1972).

50. Segretti, *supra* note 13.

51. *In re* Nixon, 53 App. Div. 2d 178, 385 N.Y.S.2d 305 (1st Dept. 1976).
52. Maryland State Bar Ass'n, Inc. v. Agnew, 271 Md. 543, 553, 318 A.2d 811, 817 (1974). *See also in re* Pearson, 17 N.J. 210, 111 A.2d 64 (1954).
53. *In re* Ward, 18 App. Div. 2d 15, 238, N.Y.S.2d 278 (4th Dept. 1963). *But see* North Carolina State Bar v. Hall, 293 N.C. 539, 238 S.E.2d 521 (1977).
54. Levy v. Association of the Bar of the City of N.Y., 37 N.Y.2d 279, 333, N.E.2d 350, 372, N.Y.S.2d 41 (1975).
55. Friday v. State Bar of Cal., 23 Cal.2d 501, 505, 144 P.2d 564, 567 (1943).
56. Nebraska State Bar Ass'n v. Holscher, 193 Neb. 729, 230 N.W.2d 75 (1975).
57. *In re* Williams, 249 Minn. 600, 83 N.W.2d 115 (1957). *See also* Annot., Attorney-Negligence-Discipline, 96 A.L.R.2d 823–92 (1964).
58. *In re* Zuber, 32 App. Div. 2d 458, 304 N.Y.S.2d 16 (2d Dept. 1969); *In re* Anonymous, 21 App. Div. 2d 48, 248 N.Y.S.2d 368 (1st Dept. 1964).
59. Wildove v. New York State Bar Ass'n, 40 App. Div. 2d 1042, 338 N.Y.S.2d 680 (3rd Dept. 1972); *In re* Brown, 45 App. Div. 2d 289, 357 N.Y.S.2d 521 (1st Dept. 1974); *In re* Zaphea, 46 App. Div. 2d 333, 362 N.Y.S.2d 468 (1st Dept. 1974); People v. Stewart, 178 Colo. 352, 497 P.2d 1003 (1972); *In re* Case, 262 Ind. 118, 311 N.E.2d 797 (1974).
60. Opinion 407, New York State Bar Ass'n. (August 28, 1975).
61. Disciplinary Rule 2-106, Code of Professional Responsibility, ABA.
62. Westchester County Bar Ass'n. v. St. John, 43 App. Div. 2d 218, 350 N.Y.S.2d 737 (2d Dept. 1974); Nebraska State Bar Ass'n v. Richards, 164 Neb. 80, 90, 84 N.W.2d 136, 143 (1957).
63. *In re* Fata, 22 App. Div. 2d 116, 254 N.Y.S.2d 289 (1st Dept. 1964), *cert. denied*, 382 U.S. 917 (1965); *In re* Gladstone, 16 App. Div. 2d 512, 229 N.Y.S.2d 663 (1st Dept. 1962).
64. Yale v. State Bar of Cal., 16 Cal.2d 175, 105 P.2d 112 (1940).
65. Disciplinary Rule 7-104(A)(2), Code of Professional Responsibility, ABA.
66. Disciplinary Rule 7-104(A)(1), Code of Professional Responsibility, ABA.
67. *Ibid.*
68. *In re* FMC Corp., 430 F. Supp. 1108 (S.D.W. Va. 1977).

69. Opinion 830, Association of the Bar of the City of New York.
70. *In re* Rook, 276 Or. 695, 556 P.2d 1351 (1976).
71. Imbler v. Pachtman, 424 U.S. 409 (1976).
72. Helstoski v. Goldstein, 552 F.2d 564 (3d Cir. 1977).
73. Federal Intermediate Credit Bank of Louisville v. Kentucky Bar Ass'n, 540 S.W.2d 14 (Ky. 1976).
74. Snyder v. State Bar of Cal., 18 Cal.3d 286, 555 P.2d 1104, 133 Cal. Rptr. 864 (1976); Committee on Professional Ethics and Conduct of Iowa State Bar Ass'n v. Roberts, —— Iowa ——, 246 N.W.2d 259 (1976).
75. Heavey v. State Bar of Cal., 17 Cal. 3d 553, 558, 551 P.2d 1238, 1241, 131 Cal. Rptr. 406, 409 (1976); Silver v. State Bar of Cal., 13 Cal.3d 134, 528 P.2d 1157, 117 Cal. Rptr. 821 (1974).
76. *In re* Albright, 274 Or. 815, 549 P.2d 527 (1976).
77. *In re* Anschell, 53 App. Div. 2d 297, 385 N.Y.S.2d 771 (1st Dept. 1976).
78. Long v. New York State Bar Ass'n, 43 App. Div. 2d 1001, 352 N.Y.S.2d 159 (3d Dept. 1974).
79. *In re* Phelps, 204 Kan. 16, 459 P.2d 172 (1969).
80. *In re* Jones, 431 S.W.2d 809 (Mo. 1966).
81. Donovan's Case, 108 N.H. 34, 226 A.2d 779 (1967).
82. *In re* Sarbone, 63 N.J. 94, 304 A.2d 734 (1973); Bar Ass'n of Baltimore v. Posner, 275 Md. 250, 339 A.2d 657 (1975); Yokozeki v. State Bar of Cal., 11 Cal.3d 436, 521 P.2d 858, 113 Cal. Rptr. 602 (1974), *cert. denied*, 419 U.S. 900 (1974).
83. *In re* Blatt, 65 N.J. 539, 324 A.2d 15 (1974).
84. Iowa State Bar Ass'n v. Kraschel, 260 Iowa 187, 148 N.W.2d 621 (1967).
85. *Ibid.*; Zitny v. State Bar of Cal., 64 Cal.2d 787, 415 P.2d 521, 51 Cal. Rptr. 825 (1966). Haray v. Blumental, 555 F.2d 1113 (2nd Cir. 1977) (different standards of proof).
86. *In re* Chipley, 254 S.C. 588, 176 S.E.2d 412 (1970), *cert. denied*, 401 U.S. 1010 (1971); *in re* Abbott, 19 Cal. 3d 249, 561 P.2d 285, 137 Cal. Rptr. 195 (1977).
87. *In re* M., 59 N.J. 304, 282 A.2d 37 (1971).
88. Florida Bar v. Worthington, 276 So.2d 39 (Fla. 1973).
89. Florida Bar v. Minkus, 285 So.2d 408 (Fla. 1973).
90. Anonymous v. New York State Bar Ass'n, 51 App. Div. 2d 340, 341, 381 N.Y.S.2d 560, 561 (4th Dept. 1976).
91. Anonymous v. New York State Bar Ass'n, 47 App. Div. 2d 83, 366 N.Y.S.2d 239 (4th Dept. 1975).
92. *In re* M., *supra* note 87.
93. *In re* Hicks, 163 Okla. 29, 20 P.2d 896 (1933).
94. *In re* Okin, 272 App. Div. 607, 73 N.Y.S.2d 861 (1st Dept. 1947).

95. *In re* Wallace, 323 Mo. 203, 19 S.W.2d 625 (1929).
96. State v. Byrkett, 4 Ohio Dec. 89, 3 Ohio N.P. 28 (1895).
97. *In re* Dibble, 257 Or. 120, 124, 478 P.2d 384, 385 (1970).
98. *In re* Gould, 4 App. Div. 2d 174, 175, 164 N.Y.S.2d 48, 49 (1st Dept. 1957).
99. *In re* Kimball, 40 App. Div. 2d 252, 255, 253, 339 N.Y.S.2d 302, 305, 303 (2d Dept. 1973).
100. *In re* Kimball, 33 N.Y.2d 586, 301 N.E.2d 436, 347 N.Y.S.2d 453 (1973). For the decision of the Florida Supreme Court disbarring Kimball, *see* Florida Bar v. Kimball, 96 So.2d 825 (Fla. 1957). For other Florida decisions disciplining attorneys because of sexual conduct, *see* Florida Bar v. Kay, 232 So.2d 378 (Fla. 1970); Florida Bar v. Hefty, 213, So.2d 422 (Fla. 1968).
101. *In re* Florida Board of Bar Examiners, 358 So.2d 7 (Fla. 1978).

IV

Lawyer Discipline – Some Procedural Issues

What constitutional rights does an attorney have at a disciplinary proceeding?

An attorney is entitled to procedural due process at a disciplinary proceeding. This includes the right to fair notice of the charges against her.[1] It also includes the opportunity to confront and cross-examine the evidence against her.[2] The attorney has the right to present evidence in her own behalf.[3] While the cited cases arise in proceedings leading to disbarment or suspension, the principles are equally applicable to cases where the attorney receives only a public censure. This is because censure carries with it a stigma which deprives the attorney of "liberty or property" within the meaning of the Fourteenth Amendment's Due Process Clause.[4]

Can an attorney ever be suspended or disbarred without a prior hearing?

Only where he has been convicted of a crime and a state law or rule makes conviction of a crime grounds for automatic suspension or disbarment.[5] At least one court, however, has indicated that even after conviction of a crime for which disbarment would otherwise follow, it is necessary to wait until the attorney has exhausted his rights of appellate review.[6]

Who has the burden of proof at a disciplinary proceeding?

The grievance committee or other prosecuting body has the burden of proof.[7] This burden requires proof of misconduct by clear and convincing evidence, in some jurisdictions.[8] Other courts have said that the burden is to prove misconduct by a preponderance of the evidence.[9] Yet other courts have said that the charges must be sustained by proof that is reasonably certain, with reasonable doubts being resolved in favor of the attorney.[10] While it has been held that the required proof is greater than in an ordinary civil action, it is generally not required that the misconduct be proved beyond a reasonable doubt.[11]

Finally, once the prosecuting authority carries its burden of proof at the formal hearing, the attorney will usually have the burden of showing a reviewing court that the disciplinary board's recommendation is erroneous or unlawful.[12]

Is an attorney charged with a disciplinary violation entitled to a jury trial?

Apparently only in Texas.[13]

Can hearsay evidence be used in a disciplinary proceeding?

In nearly all jurisdictions, only legally competent evidence is admissible.[14]

Does an attorney enjoy any presumption of innocence at a disciplinary proceeding?

Several state courts have held that he does.[15]

Are polygraph-test results admissible at a disciplinary proceeding?

While this issue has not been extensively considered, apparently not.[16]

Do any states relax the rules of evidence in disciplinary proceedings?

Yes. Arizona, for example, does not apply the "strict rules of evidence" in disciplinary proceedings. Rather, it will permit the use of evidence " 'which possesses probative value commonly accepted by reasonably prudent men in the conduct of their affairs.' "[17]

What about the use of evidence secured through illegal electronic surveillance?

It would, of course, be rather ironical if a grievance committee attempted to use illegally secured evidence to discipline an errant lawyer, but it does happen. It will not be allowed.[18]

Can an attorney assert the privilege against self-incrimination at a disciplinary proceeding? If she does, can that be used against her?

An attorney may assert her Fifth Amendment privilege against self-incrimination at a disciplinary proceeding. The fact that she does so cannot be used against her in any way and cannot be cited as a basis for disciplinary action.[19]

If a lawyer is given immunity before a federal or state grand jury and testifies, can his testimony later be used against him in a disciplinary proceeding?

Yes. All courts that have considered this question agree that the testimony given before a grand jury under a grant of immunity may nevertheless be used against the lawyer in a subsequent disciplinary proceeding. In one of the most recent cases on this subject, the New York Court of Appeals stressed that a grant of immunity protects the witness only against subsequent *criminal* prosecutions.

> Immunity does not protect against all private consequences of the facts or involvement revealed by testimony given under its shelter. . . . The criterion is whether the sanctions are imposed in the context of a criminal proceeding, covered by immunity, or whether such subsequent proceedings are civil in nature, where immunity does not necessarily extend.

The court then went on to hold that disciplinary proceedings are not "criminal proceedings but rather are those which serve to protect the court and society from the practice of law by persons who fail to maintain the necessary standards of integrity and probity."[20]

In another recent case, the United States Court of Appeals for the Seventh Circuit agreed. The fact that prior cases have called disciplinary proceedings "quasi-criminal" or "adversary" did not make them criminal cases for purposes of the Fifth Amendment. Therefore, federally immunized testimony could still be used at a state disciplinary proceeding arising out of the same events. The Seventh Circuit case is even stronger than other decisions in this area because the lawyer there, when called before the federal grand jury, was assured by his own lawyer, the federal prosecutor, and a federal district judge that his immunized testimony could *not* be used against him in a subsequent disciplinary proceeding. Yet when the state attempted to do so, the Court of Appeals held that neither the federal prosecutor nor the district judge had authority to give this assurance or immunize the use of the lawyer's testimony in a subsequent state disciplinary proceeding. The attempts to do so constituted "invalid acts." In a concurrence, one judge emphasized that he joined in the court's opinion "with considerable reluctance." He added:

> My reluctance stems from the uncomfortable feeling that there is an inherent injustice under law when a witness gives testimony under the compulsion of contempt and that testimony is to be used against him in a disciplinary proceeding which could result in a substantial penalty against him although two of the three branches of the federal government have explicitly assured the witness that the compelled testimony cannot be used against him in a disciplinary proceeding....

Nevertheless, the concurring judge concluded that the result reached by the Court was "the inexorable one under our law."[21]

But if information a lawyer gives to a grand jury under a grant of immunity can then be used against her at a disciplinary hearing, doesn't this make the right to assert the self-incrimination privilege at disciplinary hearings meaningless?

No. The right to assert the privilege against self-incrimination at a disciplinary hearing is not intended to protect the lawyer from discipline, but only the consequences of criminal prosecution. If the lawyer has already received immunity, those consequences are negated. In other words, the privilege is one against testimony that will subject the lawyer to criminal punishment, not professional discipline. Needless to add, perhaps, not many lawyers appreciate this distinction.

Does a lawyer who has been charged with a disciplinary violation have the right to appeal a decision against him?

There is no constitutional right to appeal an adverse decision. A distinction must be made. Generally, state disciplinary procedures provide for a hearing before a referee or panel. The hearing will be "on the record," that is, it will be transcribed, and the attorney will have the required procedural due-process rights at this hearing (confrontation, subpoena power, the right to be heard, etc.). The record of this hearing will be reviewed by the tribunal provided by state law with the responsibility for disciplining lawyers. As we have seen, that tribunal may or may not accept the conclusions of the hearing officer.[22] But there is no constitutional right to an appeal from a decision of that tribunal.

This is most apparent in a recent New York State case.[23] The referee at a hearing made certain factual findings favorable to the attorney charged with a disciplinary violation. Under New York practice, an intermediate appellate court of the state has the responsibility to review the referee's factual conclusions and to determine the appropriate punishment, if any. The appellate court, without ever seeing the attorney, without itself ever hearing evidence on the issues, disaffirmed certain of the factual findings of the referee and suspended the attorney. In New York, the attorney did have a right to appeal this decision to the highest state court, the Court of Appeals, but only if the appeal raised a constitutional question.[24] After the Court of Appeals declined to review the suspension, the attorney brought an action in federal district court challenging the constitutionality of the procedures used by New York in disciplining lawyers.

In addition to his claim that the procedure was unconstitutional because he did not have an opportunity to appear before the very tribunal that made the ultimate findings of fact in his case, the attorney also argued that the procedure violated his constitutional right to equal protection, since other professionals in the state who were subject to discipline did have the right to appeal to the highest state court. The court rejected all these arguments. On the last argument, it acknowledged that the intermediate state appellate court was sitting as a court of "original jurisdiction" in attorney-discipline cases and that the aggrieved attorney had no appeal right whatsoever on any but constitutional issues. Nevertheless, the court ruled that the difference in treatment between attorneys on the one hand and other professionals and other litigants on the other hand did not violate the Equal Protection Clause.[25] The United States Supreme Court affirmed.

If both criminal and disciplinary proceedings are instituted against an attorney, does he have a right to a stay of the disciplinary proceedings until the criminal charge is disposed of?

He does not have a right to a stay, although in most states the disciplinary proceeding will be voluntarily stayed until the criminal proceeding is over so as not to prejudice the criminal proceeding and because a conviction on the criminal charge will foreclose relitigating the same issues at the disciplinary proceeding. While the federal courts have the power to grant a stay if the state does not voluntarily do so, they are not likely to exercise such power.[26]

If an attorney is suspended or disbarred in a state proceeding, is he automatically suspended or disbarred in any federal court of which he may be a member?

No. State disciplinary proceedings are not binding upon the federal courts, although they are entitled to great respect.[27] Nevertheless, a federal court may choose to rely upon a state action, without holding its own hearing, if the state has complied with the following procedural due-process requirements: notice to the attorney of the charges against him and an opportunity to be heard; findings of fact that are supported by the evidence; and, in the language of one court, there is "no other 'grave reason' for ignoring the actions taken."[28]

Will the federal courts ever intervene in a state disciplinary proceeding?

Rarely. In one recent case, a claim was made that the disciplinary proceeding was brought to interfere with the lawyer's free speech rights, but the federal appellate court ruled that principles of federal-state comity required it to dismiss the lawyer's complaint. The federal court concluded that the lawyer could raise his federal constitutional claims within the state disciplinary procedure. Federal intervention while such a procedure is under way is likely to be permitted only in extraordinary circumstances, where the state proceedings have been instituted or prosecuted in bad faith or as part of a campaign of harassment, which is likely to cause irreparable injury to the attorney. Unless such a showing can be made, the mere fact that the attorney claims that the state proceeding interferes with his free speech rights will not justify federal intervention.[29]

Does it ever happen that a federal court will accept jurisdiction of an attorney's claim that he is being disciplined as a result of the exercise of his First Amendment rights?

Yes. In one recent case, an attorney was suspended from practice for six months on the ground that he had been guilty of abusive conduct and speech in four separate state court trials. He went to the federal court and alleged that the suspension violated his First Amendment rights. The federal appellate court ruled that his allegation stated a cause of action. Here, the attorney was not challenging the state disciplinary procedure or seeking to interfere with the procedure while it was underway, but made a direct claim that the suspension was intended to and did interfere with his freedom of speech.[30]

NOTES

1. *In re* Ruffalo, 390 U.S. 544 (1968); Schware v. Board of Bar Examiners of New Mexico, 353 U.S. 232 (1957).
2. Willner v. Committee on Character and Fitness, 373 U.S. 96 (1963).
3. *In re* Ginger, 372 F.2d 620 (6th Cir. 1967), *cert. denied*, 387 U.S. 935 (1967); *in re* Echeles, 430 F.2d 347 (7th Cir. 1970); *in re* Ming, 469 F.2d 1352 (7th Cir. 1972).
4. Board of Regents v. Roth, 408 U.S. 564, 573–74 (1972) (citing *Schware* and *Willner*, *supra* notes 1 and 2); Erdmann v. Stevens, 458 F.2d 1205, 1210 (2d Cir. 1972), *cert. denied*, 409 U.S. 889 (1972).
5. *In re* Kaufman, 46 App. Div. 2d 489, 363 N.Y.S.2d 324 (1st Dept. 1975).
6. *In re* Ming, *supra* note 3.
7. Charlton v. FTC, 543 F.2d 903 (D.C. Cir. 1976).
8. Louisiana State Bar Ass'n v. Brown, —— La. ——, 291 So. 2d 385 (1974); *in re* Moore, 110 Ariz. 312, 518 P.2d 562 (1974); McComb v. Commission on Judicial Performance, 19 Cal. 3d Spec. Trib. Supp. 1, 564 P.2d 1, 138 Cal. Rptr. 459 (1977).
9. *In re* Hendricks, 155 W. Va. 516, 185 S.E.2d 336 (1971) ("clear preponderance").
10. *In re* Cadwell, 15 Cal.3d 762, 543 P.2d 257, 125 Cal. Rptr. 889 (1975).
11. *In re* Phelps, 204 Kan. 16, 459 P.2d 172 (1969), *cert. denied*, 397 U.S. 916 (1970); Kentucky Bar Ass'n. v. Franklin, 534 S.W.2d 459 (Ky. 1976).
12. *In re* Honoroff, 15 Cal.3d 755, 543 P.2d 597, 126 Cal. Rptr. 229 (1975).
13. Phagan v. State, 509 S.W.2d 703 (Tex. Civ. App. 1974); McComb, *supra* note 8.
14. *In re* Echeles, *supra* note 3; *in re* Melin, 410 Ill. 332, 102 N.E.2d 119 (1951); Levy v. Association of the Bar of the City of N.Y., 37 N.Y.2d 279, 333 N.E.2d 350, 372 N.Y.S.2d 41 (1975); North Carolina State Bar v. Frazier, 269 N.C. 625, 153 S.E.2d 367 (1967); State v. Beaudry, 53 Wis. 2d 148, 191 N.W.2d 842 (1971).
15. Committee on Legal Ethics of W.V. State Bar v. Lewis, 156 W. Va. 809, 197 S.E.2d 312 (1973); *in re* Agin, 45 Ill. 2d 126, 256 N.E.2d 810 (1970); *in re* Board of

Comm'rs of Ala. State Bar v. Jones, 291 Ala. 371, 380 So. 2d 267 (1973).
16. *In re* Moyer, 77 N.M. 253, 421 P.2d 781 (1966).
17. *In re* Wilson, 76 Ariz. 49, 53, 258 P.2d 433, 436 (1953).
18. *In re* Langley, 230 Or. 319, 370 P.2d 228 (1962).
19. Spevack v. Klein, 385 U.S. 511 (1967).
20. *In re* Anonymous Attorneys, 41 N.Y.2d 506, 508–9, 362 N.E.2d 592, 595, 393 N.Y.S.2d 961, 963 (1977). The New York immunity statute grants transactional immunity to grand-jury witnesses, while the Fifth Amendment requires, and the federal courts grant only, testimonial immunity. Transactional immunity protects the witness from ever being prosecuted for the transaction about which he is forced to testify, whether or not his immunized testimony is used in the prosecution. Testimonial immunity protects the witness only from subsequent use in a criminal proceeding of his own testimony or evidence to which it may lead. Nevertheless, the result of the New York case does not depend on the fact that New York grants broader immunity than is constitutionally required, as demonstrated by the Seventh Circuit case discussed in the text and the cases in the annotation cited in note 21 below.
21. *In re* Daley, 549 F.2d 469, 481, 482 (7th Cir. 1977), *cert denied*, 434 U.S. 829 (Oct. 3, 1977). As the *Daley* court points out, state courts considering this issue have "unanimously responded" the same way. See 549 F.2d at 476 n.6. *See also Annot.*, Use in Disbarment Proceeding of Testimony Given by Attorney in Criminal Proceeding Under Grant of Immunity, 62 A.L.R.3d 1145–56 (1975).
22. Mack v. State Bar of Cal., 2 Cal.3d 440, 467 P.2d 225, 85 Cal. Rptr. 625 (1970).
23. Mildner v. Gulotta, 405 F. Supp. 182 (E.D.N.Y. 1975), *aff'd*, 425 U.S. 901 (1976).
24. N.Y. JUD. LAW. §90(8) (McKinney).
25. Mildner, *supra* note 23, 405 F. Supp. at 193–94.
26. De Vita v. Sills, 422 F.2d 1172 (3rd Cir. 1970); Huffman v. Pursue, Ltd., 420 U.S. 592 (1975).
27. *In re* Ruffalo, *supra* note 1.
28. Wrighten v. United States, 550 F.2d 990, 991 (4th Cir. 1977). *See also in re* Selling, 243 U.S. 46, 51 (1917); *in re* Rappaport, 558 F.2d 87 (2d Cir 1977).
29. Erdmann, *supra* note 4; Younger v. Harris, 401 U.S. 37 (1971). *But see* Taylor v. Kentucky State Bar Ass'n, 424 F.2d 478 (6th Cir. 1970).
30. Getty v. Reed, 547 F.2d 971 (6th Cir. 1977).

V

The Attorney-Client Relationship

What is the nature of the relationship between attorney and client, and how does it arise?

There are many sides to the attorney-client relationship. The attorney is generally considered an agent of the client.[1] She has, as the next question and answer show, a fiduciary obligation to her clients.[2]

In order to have an attorney-client relationship, it is not necessary that there be a written or formal contract between the parties. The relationship can be inferred from the conduct of the parties.[3] But although the attorney is the agent of the client, there is not created a "master and servant" relationship. In other words, the attorney does not stand in relation to the client as an employee does to an employer.[4] Indeed, one of the requirements of the Code of Professional Responsibility, set out in Canon 5, states that "a lawyer should exercise independent professional judgment on behalf of a client." He is not bound to accede to all of the wishes of the client.[5]

Although no formal contract is necessary to create the attorney-client relationship, it will not arise simply because a layman discusses the facts surrounding a particular legal problem with a lawyer. It is necessary, rather, that the attorney and the prospective client show, by words or conduct, implicitly or explicitly, that they intend to create the attorney-client relationship.[6]

For example, in one case, a man looking for a location for a sawmill approached the chairman of the Economic Development Commission for the county. The chairman also happened to be an attorney. The sawmill operator asked for assistance in locating a site for his sawmill. The chairman obliged. Eventually, there was litigation, and it was important to determine whether or not an attorney-client relationship arose between the sawmill operator and the chairman. The court concluded that it had, even though no money had been paid and no express understanding of such a relationship was entered into.[7]

While it is true in this case that even a nonlawyer could have performed the services requested of the chairman, an attorney-client relationship can arise even when the attorney is requested to do work that does not require formal legal training. In one recent case, for example, an attorney assisted in the search for a buyer for certain property. The seller subsequently tried to defeat the attorney's lien on the ground that the attorney's services did not require the skills of a lawyer and, therefore, an attorney's lien did not arise. This argument was rejected.[8]

What does it mean to say that a lawyer occupies the role of "fiduciary" in relation to a client?

The law imposes on a fiduciary relationship a greater requirement of loyalty and fair and open dealing than it does on any other legally recognized relationship. The particular demands of the lawyer-client fiduciary relationship will vary according to the purpose for which the lawyer was retained, the intelligence and worldliness of the client, other obligations of the lawyer to the courts and the adversary system of justice, and so on. But generally, the nature of the fiduciary relationship can be summarized in the language of one federal appellate court as follows:

> Implicit in every attorney-client contract is a covenant by the attorney that he will conduct himself according to customary professional standards. . . .

THE ATTORNEY-CLIENT RELATIONSHIP

> The attorney-client relationship is regarded as demanding an extremely high standard of conduct. . . . The attorney is under a duty to represent his client with the "utmost degree of honesty, forthrightness, loyalty and fidelity." . . . He must resign if at any time in the course of litigation his interests in the suit becomes "adverse or hostile to his client." . . . Hostility or adverse positions need not always be of an economic character. Indeed, custom requires that the attorney treat his clients with civility, common decency, and loyalty, both as to legal problems and as to their personal relationships.[9]

And in another recent case, the Massachusetts Supreme Court partially explained why the courts require such a high standard from lawyers:

> The attorney, like the doctor, is an expert, and much of his work is done out of the client's view. The client is not an expert; he cannot be expected to recognize professional negligence if he sees it, and he should not be expected to watch over the professional or to retain a second professional to do so. The relation of attorney and client is highly fiduciary in its nature. . . . The attorney owes his client a duty of full and fair disclosure of facts material to the client's interests.[10]

What, generally, does the client owe to the attorney?

The cases on the client's obligation to the attorney are not, as you might expect, legion. But the few that there are indicate that the relationship "is not entirely a one-way street." The relationship "envisages at the least the client's confidence in and respect for his attorney." A "wholesome regard for one's lawyer is . . . as much a part of the contract of retainer—though unwritten—as the signed agreement to pay a fee for services to be rendered." In the case just quoted, the court held that an attorney was entitled to a fee for services rendered after his client, responding to a proposed settlement which the attorney advised accepting, "became angry and abusive" and "belittled the [attorney's] capabilities as a lawyer, and told him that the only reason the settlement was recommended by the [attorney] was that he, the attorney, 'needed money very badly.'" The court ruled that this reaction amounted to a discharge without cause.[11]

Other cases hold that a client has an obligation to disclose all facts relevant to his case to his attorney and, failing to do so, cannot complain if the attorney acts improperly because he does not know the entire story.[12] Finally, while "it is incumbent upon the attorney to make himself reasonably available to his clients," a client "is under a co-equal responsibility not to complain of inaccessibility of counsel unless he has made diligent efforts to contact counsel or, due to personal or physical limitations, was unable to do so."[13]

Does a lawyer have a responsibility to keep the client informed about the progress of her case?
Yes. The ethical rules have been interpreted to require the lawyer to explain, in terms the client can understand, what the lawyer is doing in the client's behalf or why he is doing nothing.[14]

Can a lawyer who has been retained by a client give the work to another lawyer without telling the client?
No. The relationship between the attorney and the client is personal and the attorney may not assign her responsibilities to another lawyer without the client's express or implied consent.[15] On the other hand, it is obvious that when a client retains a single practitioner, it may be necessary for the attorney, during periods of occasional illness, to have another lawyer cover for her on a temporary basis. This will not violate the attorney-client relationship.[16] Finally, when a client retains an attorney who is a member of a firm, the client must expect that members of the firm other than the attorney with whom he deals may work on his case, perhaps predominantly. The client will not be able to complain about this unless there was an understanding between the attorney and the client that one or more particular attorneys would do all of the work. Likewise, where a client retains an attorney to litigate a case in a distant jurisdiction, it is obvious that the attorney will have to have local counsel.[17] Finally, if the retained

attorney does hire other counsel to assist her on a case, the client must also be informed that a division of fees will be made, although the client need not be told how the fees will be divided.[18] The fee, of course, must be divided in some rational way related to the division of services or responsibility.[19]

What is the attorney-client privilege?

The attorney-client privilege is a rule of law that protects, as confidential, communications between an attorney and a client, if these are made during the course of a professional relationship and concern the subject matter of the attorney's retainer. The purpose of the attorney-client privilege is to encourage the client to confide in his counsel. Information provided by the client or by others on behalf of the client to the attorney cannot usually be revealed without the client's agreement. The information cannot be subpoenaed. If the client or the attorney is asked in court about the contents of a confidential communication, she can decline to answer.[20]

What is the source of the rule establishing the attorney-client privilege?

In some jurisdictions, the rule is based on common law—that is, it was created by and perpetuated by the courts.[21] In other jurisdictions, the rule appears in the statutes.[22]

What if someone working in a lawyer's office learns about a confidential communication between the lawyer and the client?

If in the ordinary course of a representation of a client's interests, the lawyer reveals confidential communications to third persons for the purpose of assisting in protecting the client's interests, these communications are also privileged. The third person may not reveal what he or she has learned. This rule applies to clerks and secretaries in the lawyer's office, an accountant who may have been hired to assist the lawyer in the representation, a psychiatrist who may have been hired to aid in the preparation of a defense, and other agents of the lawyer.[23]

Does this mean that all communications between a nonlawyer and a lawyer are confidential?

Not at all. The courts have ruled that the attorney-client privilege should be narrowly construed since it is an exception to the general rule of full disclosure.[24] The following facts are usually considered in determining whether there is a lawyer-client relationship:

> 1. The asserted holder of the privilege is or sought to become a client; 2. the person to whom the communication was made (a) is a member of a bar of a court or is his subordinate and (b) in connection with this communication is acting as a lawyer; 3. the communication relates to a fact of which the attorney was informed (a) by his client (b) without the presence of strangers (c) for the purpose of securing primarily either (i) an opinion on law or (ii) legal services or (iii) assistance in some legal proceeding, and not (d) for the purpose of committing a crime or tort; 4. the privilege has been (a) claimed and (b) not waived by the client.[25]

If a client seeks business advice from his attorney, is the conversation privileged?

No. If a client hires an attorney for purely business or personal advice, as opposed to legal advice, there is no privilege.[26] In addition, simple ministerial or clerical services rendered by an attorney are not privileged. And an attorney can take action to prevent a client from going through with an announced suicide.[27]

What if a client goes to an attorney and seeks advice about a plan to commit a crime or fraud?

The conversation is not privileged and the attorney can be required to reveal it. As one court recently said, "Because the attorney-client privilege is not to be used as a cloak for illegal or fraudulent behavior, it is well established that the privilege does not apply where legal representation was secured in furtherance of intended, or present, continuing illegality." Furthermore, this exception "applies even where the attorney is completely unaware that his advice is sought in furtherance of such an improper purpose." But before the attorney can be required to reveal the contents of the communication from the client, the litigant seeking to require her to do so, usually a prosecutor, must establish that the attorney was indeed retained for an illegal or criminal purpose. Finally, it must always be remembered that the privilege only applies to communications, and not to physical evidence. If a client gives his lawyer contraband or instruments of a crime, for example, the lawyer may not hide these on the assumption that they are privileged. They are not. But the lawyer need not tell the authorities where she got them.[28]

What is the theory underlying the attorney-client privilege?

The underlying theory, and the basis for one of its exceptions, were explained in the case from the United States Court of Appeals in California cited in the last note. There, the Internal Revenue Service had served a subpoena on a law firm, requesting information from the firm with regard to payments received by it from certain clients who were under investigation for violation of internal-revenue laws. The court concluded that the government had shown that the law firm had been retained "in order to promote intended or continuing criminal or fraudulent activity, while a criminal conspiracy was already under way." As a result, the court refused to allow the attorney-client privilege to extend to the fee information sought by the Internal Revenue Service. "This is manifestly not a case," said the court, "where the attorneys were retained in order that the clients could ascertain whether or not some future course of action was lawful."

The court then described the purposes of the privilege and its limits:

> In our legal system the client should make full disclosure to the attorney so that the advice given is sound, so that the attorney can give all appropriate protection to the client's interest, and so that proper defenses are raised if litigation results. The attorney-client privilege promotes such disclosure by promising that communications revealed for these legitimate purposes will be held in strict confidence. The privi-

lege encourages persons to seek advice as to future conduct. But so important is full disclosure that the law recognizes the privilege even if the advice is sought by one who has already committed a bad act. Thus, the attorney-client privilege is central to the legal system and the adversary process. For these reasons, the privilege may deserve unique protection in the courts. But a *quid pro quo* is exacted for the attorney-client confidence: the client must not abuse the confidential relation by using it to further a fraudulent or criminal scheme, and as a condition to continued representation, the lawyer is required to advise the client to cease any unlawful activities that the lawyer perceives are occurring. Law and society consent to the attorney-client privilege on these preconditions. By insisting on their observance, we safeguard the privilege itself and protect the integrity of the professional relation.[29]

What happens if a third person who is not an agent or employee of the attorney is present when the confidential communication is revealed?

Then the privilege is lost and the attorney or client can be forced to reveal their conversation.[30] Nevertheless, the courts will carefully inspect the circumstances under which the third person was present to determine whether the privilege should be destroyed.[31] One important exception to this rule is that where several clients are involved in a litigation and they meet with their attorneys to plan their case, the conversation is privileged.[32]

Are there any types of information that are not privileged even though they arise during an otherwise valid attorney-client relationship?

Yes. Generally, the *fact* that there is an attorney-client relationship and the specific authorization for its creation are not privileged subjects.[33] The general rule is also that the attorney-client privilege does not protect the client's name or the amount of fee actually paid.[34] An exception is sometimes made where the very existence of an attorney-client relationship could incriminate the client.[35] The attorney's perception of the client's mental competency is also not privileged so long as the attorney does not reveal the subject of any communications between him and the client.[36] The attorney can be required to reveal the general nature of the services for which he was retained.[37] Finally, a lawyer may reveal confidential information if that is necessary in order to adequately defend himself against an accusation of wrongdoing.[38]

Are communications between an attorney and a corporate client protected by an attorney-client privilege?

Yes. In the early 1960s, a federal judge in Illinois ruled that such communications were *not* privileged. Hundreds of terrified lawyers participated in an appeal to the United States Court of Appeals for the Seventh Circuit, challenging this ruling. The Court of Appeals concluded that the privilege did apply to communications between an attorney and a corporate client.[39]

Can the attorney claim the attorney-client privilege even if the client doesn't want to?

No. While the attorney may assert the privilege in the first instance,[40] the privilege belongs to the client, not the attorney. If the client wants to waive the privilege, she is free to do so.[41]

Has a client's identity ever been held to be privileged?

Yes, in situations where the revelation of the client's identity would subject the client to criminal prosecution, for example. In one case, certain attorneys for a number of taxpayers came to the office of a lawyer named Baird. The attorneys gave Baird more than $12,000 and instructed him to send this sum to the Internal Revenue Service on behalf of the taxpayers, who were not identified to the IRS and whose identity, in fact, Baird himself did not know. There was no current IRS investigation. The IRS attempted to learn the identity of the attorneys who had approached Baird. The Ninth Circuit Court of Appeals ruled that this information was privileged.[42] The Seventh Circuit has taken a similar position.[43]

In another case, a lawyer had been called before a federal grand jury in New York and asked for the address and telephone number of one of his clients. The purpose of the inquiry was to assist the Federal Bureau of Investigation in locating the client so that FBI agents could ask the client about the whereabouts of a third person. The attorney had offered to make his client available for questioning by the FBI, but did not want to reveal his client's address and phone number. The government rejected this offer and subpoenaed the attorney before the grand jury. The federal district court ruled that the government's action was an abuse of the grand-jury process and quashed the subpoena.[44]

Finally, in a New York case, a client gave his attorney certain information to be turned over to the New York City Commissioner of Investigation. The Commissioner of Investigation subpoenaed the attorney and asked the name of his client. The attorney refused to give it. The highest state court held that it was improper to hold the attorney in contempt for failure to reveal his client's identity.[45]

What happens after the attorney-client relationship ends?

Even after the attorney-client relationship ends, privileged information remains privileged, as long as the privilege is not waived or another exception does not come into play.[46] The attorney-client privilege is waived if the client attacks the competence of his attorney or in some other way challenges his lawyer's effectiveness.[47]

What authority does an attorney have to act for her client?

Like any other agent, an attorney has the authority to act for and bind her client within the scope of the attorney's retainer—that which she was hired to do. In some states the attorney can make some pretty important decisions at trial even if the client disagrees, though the attorney may first have to consult the client.[48]

What happens if the attorney intentionally or by mistake does something the client doesn't want him to do?

The client will still be bound by the attorney's acts if they are within the scope of the retainer, but the client may be able to sue the attorney for malpractice. This is because the people with whom the attorney is dealing on behalf of the client do not know that the attorney may be unauthorized to take the particular action he has. As far as they are concerned, the attorney has what lawyers call "apparent authority" to do what he is doing. Accordingly, the attorney can bind his client to the action he takes on behalf of his client, even if the client disapproves of the action.[49]

Are there any exceptions to this?

Sometimes, and in some courts. For example, an attorney may validly waive a criminal defendant's constitutional rights if he believes that the waiver will give the client a tactical advantage.[50] But he may not do so over the express disagreement of the client.[51] An attorney's acts only bind the client if they are made in the course of the attorney's retainer.[52] An attorney is only empowered to act on behalf of his *client,* so in order for the authority to exist there must be an attorney-client relationship.[53] Finally, an attorney may not settle or compromise a client's cause without the client's express authority. The mere fact that the client has retained the attorney to prosecute or defend in a litigation does not give the attorney the right to settle it without the client's approval.[54]

Can the client settle the action without the attorney's approval?

Yes. As one court recently said: The claim belongs to the client and not the attorney; the client has the right to compromise or even abandon his claim if he sees fit to do so. Furthermore, the client can settle or abandon his claim even if he has entered into a separate agreement with the attorney not to do so without the attorney's consent.[55]

If a client settles a claim without the attorney's agreement, will the client owe the attorney money for work done?

Yes, unless the client had good cause to discharge the attorney. In other words, the client has the power to decide to settle the claim, but he still has the obligation to pay his lawyer.[56]

What other acts does a client give or not give an attorney authority to perform merely by virtue of a retainer?

Without express authority, a lawyer cannot endorse a negotiable instrument on behalf of a client or assign a client's property.[57] An attorney may be given actual or apparent authority to contractually bind a client to another.[58] An attorney generally may not, without express authority, agree to the entry of a consent judgment against a client.[59] An attorney can bind his client to stipulations or admissions of fact.[60] A criminal defendant is bound by his lawyer's trial tactics and judgment in the conduct of a defense, unless it can be shown that the attorney was not acting in the client's best interests.[61] The attorney, not the client, is in charge of the conduct of a litigation, even if the client does not fully understand what is going on.[62] An attorney with authority to settle a claim also has authority to receive the settlement money. Payment of the money to the attorney discharges the claim even if the attorney never pays the money to the client.[63]

What happens if a lawyer settles a client's action without his consent?

In most states, a lawyer will need express or implied authority before she can settle an action; if she doesn't have that authority, the settlement will have no force. A client does not provide his lawyer with authority to settle an action or compromise a claim merely because the client hires the lawyer to litigate the action or claim.[64] In some states, even implied authority is not sufficient to permit a lawyer to settle a claim; express authority is required.[65] So if the lawyer settles an action without implied, and in some places express, authority, the client will not be bound by the settlement.

How can the attorney-client relationship end?

In a lot of ways. The parties can agree to terminate it.[66] Either party can terminate the relationship for cause.[67] The client can terminate the relationship without cause so long as there is no undue prejudice to his adversary or the administration of justice, although the attorney's fee, if he is entitled to a fee, may have to be protected.[68] If the attorney is disbarred, the relationship ends.[69] If the attorney is suspended, the relationship ends.[70] The death of either the client or the attorney will terminate the relationship.[71] If the client is a corporation or a partnership and it dissolves, the relationship will be terminated.[72] If either the attorney or the client becomes insane, the relationship is terminated.[73] Finally, if the purpose for which the client has retained the attorney is completed, the attorney-client relationship will also end.[74]

Does this mean a client can fire his lawyer?

A client has the right to change attorneys at any time, with a few limitations. A client may not use the pretext of changing attorneys in order to unduly delay a trial or proceeding. He may not change attorneys if the change will unfairly prejudice another party to the litigation or interfere with the administration of justice. Furthermore, there may be times when an attorney, under a valid agreement with a client, has an interest in the subject matter of the litigation. In such rare cases, the client may be prevented from changing attorneys.[75]

If the client fires a lawyer, what about the attorney's fee for work already done?

If a client discharges her attorney without cause—that is, without a good legal reason to do so—she will be liable to the attorney for the value of the work the attorney has already done. It may be that the court will not allow the client to discharge the attorney until the attorney is paid or her fee is otherwise secured.[76] One way of assuring that the attorney's fee is secured is through a lien, which we will discuss in Chapter VII.[77] If the client claims that she is discharging her attorney for cause, the court will generally defer the issue of fee until there can be a hearing on the matter.[78]

What constitutes "cause" justifying a client to fire her lawyer?

Many things. Most of them are discussed throughout this book. For example, if the attorney does something unethical with regard to the client, if she is suspended or disbarred, if she does a professionally poor job on the client's case (see Chapter VIII on malpractice), if she has a conflict of interests (see Chapter VI), or if she asks to end the representation, all provide cause for discharge.

What constitutes good cause for an attorney to withdraw from a case?

An assigned attorney may withdraw from a criminal case if he concludes that the client's position is frivolous.[79] Where an attorney receives conflicting instructions from a client, after a client has made inconsistent statements in two lawsuits, he may move to withdraw.[80] Where the attorney and the client have a basic disagreement about the strategy of the litigation, the attorney may be permitted to withdraw.[81] Where there is a conflict of interest between the attorney and the client, withdrawal will be allowed.[82] If the attorney realizes he will have to testify at the trial as a witness, he should be permitted to withdraw.[83] Where an attorney represents an insurer in the defense of an insured defendant and the insurer later concludes that the insurance policy does not cover the alleged liability, the attorney may be permitted to withdraw.[84]

Can an attorney withdraw from a case just because a client does not accept her advice to settle?

No. The client controls the decision whether and for how much to settle. And this decision binds the attorney even though she may disagree. The client's decision to settle or not to settle is not a ground for withdrawal by the attorney. Nor is it adequate that the case turns out to be less profitable than the attorney anticipated. If an attorney withdraws for any of these reasons, her withdrawal will be without cause and she will forfeit her attorney's lien.[85] See Chapter VII for more cases.

Can an attorney withdraw if his client fails to pay him?

Yes, so long as the withdrawal does not interfere with the administration of justice and the attorney does not unreasonably delay before making a motion to withdraw. The attorney does not have an absolute right to withdraw for nonpayment; rather, permission is in the discretion of the court.[86]

THE ATTORNEY-CLIENT RELATIONSHIP

What if a client hires an attorney who is a member of a law firm and the attorney later dies or leaves the firm?

If it was clear that the client was hiring the particular attorney to give the client's matter her personal attention, then a client will have the option of terminating the relationship with the law firm without penalty except that the client will have to pay the firm for the reasonable value of its services until then. The law firm, on the other hand, does not have the option of terminating the relationship with the client, but rather has an obligation to complete the legal work for which the firm had been retained, if the client so wishes.[87]

NOTES

1. Brinkley v. Farmers Elevator Mutual Insurance Co., 485 F.2d 1283 (10th Cir. 1973); Committee on Prof. Ethics and Grievances of V.I. Bar Ass'n v. Johnson, 447 F.2d 169 (3d Cir. 1971); Rolfstad, Winkjer, Suess, McKennett and Kaiser, P.C. v. Hanson, 221 N.W.2d 734 (N.D. 1974); C.C. Plumb Mixes, Inc. v. Stone, 108 R.I. 75, 272 A.2d 152 (1971); Novak v. City of Delavan, 31 Wis.2d 200, 143 N.W.2d 6 (1966).
2. Dresden v. Willock, 518 F.2d 281 (3d Cir. 1975); Sodikoff v. State Bar of Cal., 14 Cal.3d 422, 535 P.2d 331, 121 Cal. Rptr. 467 (1975); *in re* Czachorski, 41 Ill.2d 549, 244 N.E.2d 164 (1969); McMahon v. Pfister, 39 App. Div. 2d 691, 332 N.Y.S.2d 591 (1st Dept. 1972); *in re* Bretz, 168 Mont. 23, 542 P.2d 1227 (1975); Hafter v. Farkas, 498 F.2d 587 (2d Cir. 1974).
3. Farnham v. State Bar of Cal., 17 Cal.3d 605, 552 P.2d 44, 131 Cal. Rptr. 661 (1976); E.F. Hutton & Co., Inc. v. Brown, 305 F. Supp. 371 (S.D. Tex. 1969).
4. Sams v. Olah, 225 Ga. 497, 169 S.E.2d 790 (1969), *cert. denied*, 397 U.S. 914 (1970).
5. *In re* King, 133 Vt. 245, 336 A.2d 195 (1975).
6. Manuel v. Salisbury, 446 F.2d 453 (6th Cir. 1971), *cert. denied*, 405 U.S. 1046 (1972); Committee on Prof. Ethics and Grievances of V.I. Bar Ass'n, *supra* note 1.
7. Huester v. Clements, 252 Md. 641, 250 A.2d 855 (1969).
8. First National Bank of Cincinnati v. Pepper, 547 F.2d 708 (2d Cir. 1976).

9. Singleton v. Foreman, 435 F.2d 962, 970 (5th Cir. 1970).
10. Hendrickson v. Sears, 365 Mass. 83, 310 N.E.2d 131, 135 (1974).
11. Matarrese v. Wilson, 202 Misc. 994, 997, 118 N.Y.S.2d 5, 8 (Sup. Ct. Bronx County 1952).
12. Tool Research & Engineering Corp. v. Henigson, 46 Cal. App. 3d 675, 120 Cal. Rptr. 291 (1975).
13. State v. Pflieger, 15 Or. App. 383, 515 P.2d 1348, 1351 (1973).
14. Cleveland Bar Ass'n v. O'Malley, 12 Ohio St. 2d 35, 231 N.E.2d 311 (1967).
15. People v. Betillo, 53 Misc. 2d 540, 546, 279 N.Y.S.2d 444, 453 (Sup. Ct. N.Y. County 1967); Palmer v. Breyfogle, 217 Kan. 128, 535 P.2d 955 (1975).
16. Koehler v. Wales, 16 Wash. App. 304, 556 P.2d 233 (1976).
17. *See* Atlantic & Gulf Stevedores, Inc. v. Kominers, 456 F.2d 1146 (2d Cir. 1972).
18. Palmer, *supra* note 15; Schroeder v. Schaefer, 258 Or. 444, 477 P.2d 720 (1970), *modified*, 258 Or. 444, 483 P.2d 818 (1971).
19. Disciplinary Rule 2-107, Code of Professional Responsibility, ABA.
20. United States v. Goldfarb, 328 F.2d 280 (6th Cir. 1964), *cert. denied*, 377 U.S. 976 (1964); Continental Oil Co. v. United States, 330 F.2d 347 (9th Cir. 1964); United States v. Alvarez, 519 F.2d 1036 (3d Cir. 1975).
21. United States v. Tratner, 511 F.2d 248 (7th Cir. 1975); FED. R. EVID. 501.
22. New York C.P.L.R. 4503(a); MINN. STAT. ANN. § 595.02.
23. United States v. Kovel, 296 F.2d 918 (2d Cir. 1961); United States v. Alvarez, *supra* note 20; United States v. Pipkins, 528 F.2d 559 (5th Cir. 1976), *cert. denied*, 426 U.S. 952 (1976); *in re* Glines 16 App. Div. 2d 743, 227 N.Y.S.2d 71 (4th Dept. 1962) (lawyer's secretary could not disclose privileged communications, but could testify on the terms of a contract for legal services between attorney and decedent and could also reveal the services actually performed).
24. *In re* Horowitz, 482 F.2d 72 (2d Cir. 1973), *cert. denied*, 414 U.S. 867 (1973); United States v. Goldfarb, *supra* note 20.
25. United States v. United Shoe Mach. Corp., 89 F. Supp. 357, 358–59 (D. Mass. 1950), *aff'd*, 347 U.S. 521 (1954); *in re* Grand Jury Proceedings, 517 F.2d 666 (5th Cir. 1975).

26. Radiant Burners, Inc. v. American Gas Ass'n, 320 F.2d 314 (7th Cir. 1963), *cert. denied,* 375 U.S. 929 (1963); United States v. Calvert, 523 F.2d 895 (8th Cir. 1975), *cert. denied,* 424 U.S. 911 (1976).
27. United States v. Bartone, 400 F.2d 459 (6th Cir. 1968), *cert. denied,* 393 U.S. 1027 (1969). Op. No. 486, N.Y.S. Bar. Assoc. (June 19, 1978).
28. United States v. Hodge and Zweig, 548 F.2d 1347, 1354 (9th Cir. 1977); United States v. Aldridge, 484 F.2d 655 7th Cir. 1973), *cert. denied,* 415 U.S. 960 (1974); Duplan Corp. v. Deering Milliken, Inc., 397 F. Supp. 1146 (1975) (tortious conduct destroys privilege.) *In re* Ryder, 263 F. Supp. 360 (E.D. Va. 1967) (instruments of crime) *aff'd* 381 F.2d 713 (4th Cir. 1967).
29. United States v. Hodge and Zweig, *supra* note 28, at 1347, 1355.
30. United States v. Blackburn, 446 F.2d 1089 (5th Cir. 1971), *cert. denied,* 404 U.S. 1017 (1972).
31. United States v. Bigos, 459 F.2d 639 (1st Cir. 1972), *cert. denied,* 409 U.S. 847 (1972).
32. Hunydee v. United States, 355 F.2d 183 (9th Cir. 1965); *in re* Grand Jury Subpoena, 406 F. Supp. 381 (S.D.N.Y. 1975) (holding that information revealed during joint defense conference, while privileged as between the conferees and all others, can be used by any of the clients present against the other clients in the event of a subsequent controvery between them). Matter of Friedman, 64 App. Div. 2d 70, —— N.Y.S.2d —— (Dept. 1978) (privilege does not apply in subsequent litigation between the parties jointly consulting the attorney).
33. National Union Fire Insurance Co. of Pittsburgh v. Aetna Casualty & Surety Co., 384 F.2d 316 (D.C. Cir. 1967).
34. Wirtz v. Fowler, 372 F.2d 315 (5th Cir. 1966); Howell v. Jones, 516 F.2d 53 (5th Cir. 1975), *cert. denied,* 424 U.S. 916 (1976); *in re* Semel, 411 F.2d 195 (3d Cir. 1969), *cert. denied,* 396 U.S. 905 (1969).
35. *In re* Michaelson, 511 F.2d 882 (9th Cir. 1975), *cert. denied,* 421 U.S. 978 (1975).
36. United States v. Kendrick, 331 F.2d 110 (4th Cir. 1964).
37. United States v. Mackey, 405 F. Supp. 854 (E.D.N.Y. 1975).
38. Meyerhofer v. Empire Fire & Marine Insurance Co., 497 F.2d 1190 (2d Cir. 1974), *cert. denied,* 419 U.S. 998 (1974).
39. Radiant Burners, Inc., *supra* note 26.

40. Fisher v. United States, 425 U.S. 391 (1976).
41. Republic Gear Co. v. Borg-Warner Corp., 381 F.2d 551 (2d Cir. 1967).
42. Baird v. Koerner, 279 F.2d 623 (9th Cir. 1960).
43. Tillotson v. Boughner, 350 F.2d 663 (7th Cir. 1965).
44. *In re* Stolar, 397 F. Supp. 520 (S.D.N.Y. 1975). *See also in re* Grand Jury Subpoenas Served upon Field, 408 F. Supp. 1169 (S.D.N.Y. 1976). *Cf. in re* Kinoy, 326 F. Supp. 400 (S.D.N.Y. 1970).
45. *In re* Kaplan, 8 N.Y.2d 214, 168 N.E.2d 660, 203 N.Y.S.2d 836 (1960). *But see* Banco Frances e Brasileiro S.A. v. Doe, 36 N.Y.2d 592, 331 N.E.2d 502, 370 N.Y.S.2d 534 (1975), *cert. denied,* 423 U.S. 867 (1975).
46. American Can Co., v. Citrus Feed Co., 436 F.2d 1125 (5th Cir. 1971).
47. Tasby v. United States, 504 F.2d 332 (8th Cir. 1974), *cert. denied,* 419 U.S. 1125 (1975).
48. McGinnis v. Chance, 247 Md. 393, 231 A.2d 63 (1967); Paras v. City of Portsmouth, 115 N.H. 63, 335 A.2d 304 (1975); Davis v. United Fruit Co., 402 F.2d 328 (2d Cir. 1968), *cert. denied,* 393 U.S. 1085 (1969). State v. Ames, —— Kan. ——, 563 P.2d 1034 (1977) (attorney's authority at trial).
49. Ricks v. Teslow Consol., 162 Mont. 469, 512 P.2d 1304 (1973); Paras, *supra* note 48; King v. Brown, 103 R.I. 154, 235 A.2d 874 (1967); Hucks v. Green's Fuel of S.C., 247 S.C. 457, 148 S.E.2d 149 (1966).
50. United States v. Marcello, 423 F.2d 993 (5th Cir. 1970), *cert. denied,* 398 U.S. 959 (1970). *Cf.* Wainwright v. Sykes, 433 U.S. 72 (1977).
51. Brookhart v. Janis, 384 U.S. 1 (1966).
52. Vaccaro v. Alcoa Steamship Co., 405 F.2d 1133 (2d Cir. 1968); State *ex rel.* State Eng. v. Crider, 78 N.M. 312, 431 P.2d 45 (1967).
53. *In re* Wisconsin Pub. Serv. Corp., 66 Wis.2d 620, 225 N.W.2d 488 (1975); Sinnott v. Porter, 57 Wis.2d 462, 204 N.W.2d 449 (1973).
54. Clarion Corp. v. American Home Prods. Corp., 494 F.2d 860 (7th Cir. 1974), *cert. denied,* 419 U.S. 870 (1974); Singleton v. Foreman, 435 F.2d 962 (5th Cir. 1970); Thomas v. Colorado Trust Deed Funds, Inc., 366 F.2d 136 (10th Cir. 1966); Navrides v. Zurich Ins. Co., 5 Cal.3d 698, 488 P.2d 637, 97 Cal. Rptr. 309 (1971); Morr v. Crouch, 19 Ohio St. 2d 24, 249 N.E.2d 780 (1969).
55. Knoll v. Klatt, 43 Wis.2d 265, 271, 168 N.W.2d 555, 558–59 (1969); Dew v. Requa, 218 Ark. 911, 239 S.W.2d

603 (1951); Jones v. Jones, 117 Colo. 420, 188 P.2d 892 (1948).
56. Knoll, *supra* note 55.
57. Navrides, *supra* note 54; *in re* Ullman's Estate, 56 Misc. 2d 495, 289 N.Y.S.2d 833 (N.Y. Co. 1968).
58. Central N.Y. Realty Corp. v. Abel, 28 App. Div. 2d 50, 281 N.Y.S.2d 115 (4th Dept. 1967), *aff'd*, 22 N.Y. 2d 963, 242 N.E. 2d 484, 295 N.Y.S. 2d 332 (1968).
59. Associates Disc. Corp. v. Goldman, 524 F.2d 1051 (3d Cir. 1975). *But see* Eida v. Stoddard, 111 N.H. 123, 276 A.2d 12 (1971).
60. United States v. Adams, 422 F.2d 515 (10th Cir. 1970), *cert. denied*, 399 U.S. 913 (1970) (during trial); United States v. Cravero, 530 F.2d 666 (5th Cir. 1976) (during trial); Meyer v. Meyer, 209 Kan. 31, 495 P.2d 942 (1972); Prince Georges Props., Inc. v. Rogers, 275 Md. 582, 341 A.2d 804 (1975); Venizelos v. Venizelos, 30 App. Div. 2d 856, 293 N.Y.S.2d 20 (2d Dept. 1968); State *ex rel*. Davis v. Higgs, 28 Utah 2d 428, 503 P.2d 1206 (1972).
61. Poole v. Fitzharris, 396 F.2d 544 (9th Cir. 1968); United States v. Meek, 388 F.2d 936 (7th Cir. 1968), *cert. denied*, 391 U.S. 951 (1968); United States *ex rel*. Cruz v. LaVallee, 448 F.2d 671 (2d Cir. 1971), *cert. denied*, 406 U.S. 958 (1972); State v. Blanchey, 75 Wash. 2d 926, 454 P.2d 841 (1969), *cert. denied*, 396 U.S. 1045 (1970); State v. Ames, 222 Kan. 88, 563 P.2d 1034 (1977).
62. Burt v. Gahan, 351 Mass. 340, 220 N.E.2d 817 (1966); Eida, *supra* note 59; Adams v. Commonwealth, 424 S.W.2d 849 (Ky. 1968); State v. Robinson, 290 N.C. 56, 224 S.E.2d 174 (1976); State v. Reid, 114 Ariz. 16, 559 P.2d 136 (1976), *cert. denied*, U.S. (1977); Salesian Soc'y, Inc. v. Village of Ellenville, 41 N.Y.2d 521; 362 N.E.2d 604, 393 N.Y.S.2d 972 (1977). *Cf*. Wainwright, *supra*, note 50.
63. Navrides, *supra* note 54; Hutzler v. Hertz Corp., 39 N.Y.2d 209, 347 N.E.2d 627, 383 N.Y.S.2d 266 (1976).
64. Morr, *supra* note 54.
65. Harrop v. Western Airlines, Inc., 550 F.2d 1143 (9th Cir. 1977); Accrocco v. Splawn, 264 Md. 527, 287 A.2d 275 (1972).
66. Tormo v. Yormark, 398 F. Supp. 1159 (D.N.J. 1975).
67. Goldsmith v. Pyramid Communications, Inc., 362 F. Supp. 694 (S.D.N.Y. 1973); Coclin Tobacco Co. v. Griswold, 408 F.2d 1338 (1st Cir. 1969), *cert. denied*, 396 U.S. 940 (1969).

68. Fracasse v. Brent, 6 Cal.3d 784, 494 P.2d 9, 100 Cal. Rptr. 385 (1972); *in re* Phelps, 204 Kan. 16, 459 P.2d 172 (1969); Paolillo v. American Export Isbrandtsen Lines, Inc., 305 F. Supp. 250 (S.D.N.Y. 1969).
69. Ginger v. Cohn, 426 F.2d 1385 (6th Cir. 1970); Mattera v. New York Central R.R., 2 App. Div. 2d 865, 156 N.Y.S.2d 164 (2d Dept. 1956).
70. Antonsen v. Pacific Container Co., 48 Cal. App. 2d 535, 120 P.2d 148 (1941).
71. Brown v. Roberts, —— Iowa ——, 205 N.W.2d 746 (1973); Canter v. Aranow, 181 Misc. 947, 50 N.Y.S.2d 397 (Sup. Ct. 1944), *aff'd*, 269 App. Div. 668, 53 N.Y.S.2d 471 (2d Dept. 1945).
72. Fessler v. Weiss, 348 Ill. App. 21, 107 N.E.2d 795 (1952).
73. Donnelly v. Parker, 486 F.2d 402 (D.C. Cir. 1973); Corson v. Lewis, 77 Neb. 446, 109 N.W. 735 (1906).
74. Flores v. State, 79 N.M. 47, 439 P.2d 565 (1968) (holding also that acceptance of judicial office terminates attorney-client relationship); Tormo, *supra* note 66.
75. Butterman v. Walston & Co., 387 F.2d 822 (7th Cir. 1967), *cert. denied*, 391 U.S. 913 (1968); Walsh v. O'Neill, 350 Mass. 586, 215 N.E.2d 915 (1966); *in re* Estate of Ainsworth, 52 Wis. 2d 152, 187 N.W.2d 828 (1971).
76. Iowa v. Union Asphalt & Roadoils Inc., 281 F. Supp. 391 (S.D. Iowa 1968), *aff'd sub nom*. Standard Oil Co. v. Iowa, 408 F.2d 1171 (8th Cir. 1969), *aff'd*, 409 F.2d 1239 (8th Cir. 1969); City of Hankinson v. Otter Tail Power Co., 294 F. Supp. 249 (D.N.D. 1969).
77. Carroll v. Miyashiro, 50 Haw. 413, 441 P.2d 638 (1968); Shelbourne Garage, Inc. v. Licht, 34 App. Div. 2d 563, 309 N.Y.S.2d 850 (2d Dept. 1970).
78. Kaplan v. Shell Oil Co., 50 App. Div. 2d 598, 375 N.Y.S.2d 370 (2d Dept. 1975).
79. Anders v. Cal., 386 U.S. 738 (1967).
80. Knapp v. McFarland, 457 F.2d 881 (2d Cir. 1972), *cert. denied*, 409 U.S. 850 (1972).
81. Goldsmith, *supra* note 67; Imhoff v. Hammer, ——Del. ——, 305 A.2d 325 (1973).
82. Allen v. District Court, Tenth Jud. Dist., 184 Colo. 202, 519 P.2d 351 (1974).
83. Bosley v. Grand Lodge of Masons of Md., 263 Md. 303, 283 A.2d 587 (1971), *cert. denied*, 409 U.S. 844 (1972).
84. Tartaglia v. DeAragon, 52 App. Div. 2d 876, 383 N.Y.S.2d 54 (2d Dept. 1976). *See also* A.B.A. Code of Pr. Resp. DR 2-110.

85. Suffolk Roadways, Inc. v. Minuse, 56 Misc.2d 6, 287 N.Y.S.2d 965 (Sup. Ct. Suffolk County 1968). *See also* Borup v. National Airlines, Inc., 159 F. Supp. 808 (S.D.N.Y. 1958).
86. Jacobs v. Pendel, 98 N.J. Super. 252, 236 A.2d 888 (App. Div. 1967).
87. Creason v. Harding, 344 Mo. 452, 126 S.W.2d 1179 (1939).

VI

Conflicts of Interest

Can a lawyer represent opposing interests, or clients who are to some extent adverse to each other?

Sometimes. This is a complicated area. The starting points are Disciplinary Rules 5-105(A) and (B), which, in substance, prohibit a lawyer from accepting employment or continuing with multiple employment if, in either case, the exercise of the lawyer's independent professional judgment in behalf of the client will be or is likely to be adversely affected. Furthermore, Canon 9 says that "a lawyer should avoid even the appearance of professional impropriety." Therefore, even if the lawyer concludes that his professional judgment will not be adversely affected through multiple representations, he may nevertheless be required to decline such representations if accepting them conveys the appearance of impropriety. Finally, Disciplinary Rule 9-101(B) states: "A lawyer shall not accept private employment in a matter in which he had substantial responsibility while he was a public employee."

Obviously, these rules are general and do not always indicate the clear resolution where a conflict of interest is charged. To add to the confusion, Disciplinary Rule 5-

105(C) makes an exception. It allows a lawyer to represent "multiple clients if it is obvious that he can adequately represent the interest of each and if each consents to the representation after full disclosure of the possible effect of such representation on the exercise of his independent professional judgment on behalf of each."

Why can't lawyers represent conflicting interests?

The simple answer is that a lawyer owes duties of loyalty and confidentiality to a client. If she represents clients whose interests do or may conflict, she will be in the position of having to honor her duties of loyalty and confidentiality to one client at the expense of another. Of course, if there is no attorney-client relationship with a particular person, there is no duty of loyalty and confidentiality and the lawyer is free to represent interests adverse to that person.[1]

What does it mean to say that a lawyer should avoid even the appearance of professional impropriety?

Canon 9 of the Code of Professional Responsibility requires a lawyer to avoid even the appearance of impropriety. This means that the lawyer should not undertake a representation where, to other reasonable people unfamiliar with all of the facts, it appears that the lawyer is doing something unprofessional, such as arguing for opposing interests or using confidential information. It does not matter that the lawyer in fact is not doing anything actually improper. The appearance of propriety is thought also to be important because it assures confidence in the administration of justice. As one court wrote, "No practice must be permitted to prevail which invites towards the administration of justice a doubt or distrust of its integrity."[2]

Can a lawyer represent someone who is suing a former client of that lawyer?

Yes, under certain circumstances. Much depends upon the nature and form of the prior representation. For example, in one recent case, a young lawyer worked at a large California law firm which represented Shell Oil Company and the Exxon Corporation. Later he went to work for a smaller firm in California. The new firm subsequently represented a plaintiff in an action against Shell and Exxon. Shell and Exxon made motions to disqualify the new firm from representing the plaintiff. They argued that since the young lawyer had previously worked for the large firm that represented them, his presence on the staff of the new firm disqualified the new law firm from bringing the action. The court ruled otherwise. It pointed out that although the young lawyer did in fact represent Shell and Exxon while he was working for the large law firm, he never represented either company on the issues involved in the current litigation. And while it was true that the young lawyer had physical access to all of the Exxon and Shell files when he was at the large firm, the proof showed that in fact he never examined those files dealing with the current litigation. In short, he had no *actual* access to confidential information relating to the current lawsuit.[3]

In another case, on the other hand, a lawyer representing certain plaintiffs sued for a judicial declaration that patents owned by the defendant were invalid. The defendant sought to disqualify the lawyer on the ground that he had previously represented a part-owner of the defendant in litigation where the issue was identical—the validity of the patents. The court disqualified the lawyer. In doing so, the court wrote that unless the representation was forbidden in cases like this,

> a client would hardly be inclined to discuss his problems freely and in depth with his lawyer, for he would justifiably fear that information he reveals to his lawyer on one day may be used against him on the next. . . . Even the most rigorous self-discipline might not prevent a lawyer from unconsciously using or manipulating a confidence acquired in the earlier representation and transforming it into a telling advantage in the subsequent litigation. . . . These considerations require application of a strict prophylactic rule to prevent any possibility, however slight, that confidential information acquired from a client during a previous relationship may subsequently be used to the client's disadvantage.

Furthermore, the court would not hold a hearing to determine whether in fact confidential information was passed. Such a hearing would itself interfere with confidentiality. On the contrary, where it can reasonably be said that in the course of the former representation the attorney *might* have acquired information related to the subject matter of his subsequent representation, the attorney will be disqualified.[4]

Does the creation of a "prophylactic rule" mean that whenever a lawyer has previously worked on a case for a client, he can never sue the client?

Not exactly. The rule requires that there be some *substantial relationship* between the work the attorney may have done for the former client and the subject matter of the current litigation. If that can be shown, and the former client does not waive the conflict, disqualification is automatic, since the court will not inquire into whether confidential information acquired by the attorney during his former representation is actually being used in the current litigation.[5] On the other hand, disqualification will not follow if the prior representation is not substantially related to the subject matter of the current litigation, or if there was no expectation that information transmitted in the former representation would be confidential.[6]

Remember, too, that a special problem arises with regard to large law firms. Since these firms have many young lawyers as employees, or associates, and since they represent many large corporations, a strict application of the disqualification rules would prohibit any law firm that might employ a former associate from a large firm from ever suing any of the large firm's clients. Since these clients can run into the hundreds, and since a smaller firm might employ former associates from several different large firms, disqualification can be quite burdensome. As we saw in the case involving Shell Oil and Exxon, discussed above, the courts will not automatically disqualify a firm because it employs a person who formerly worked for another firm which is representing a party in the current litigation. It will have to be shown that the former associate had actual (not potential) access to confidential information. It is not enough that confidential information

CONFLICTS OF INTEREST

was present in the file room of his former employer and he theoretically had access to it.[7]

We have been discussing cases in which an attorney sues a former client. What if an attorney sues a current client?

This will rarely if ever be tolerated. The "substantial relationship" test does not apply in the case of a current client. That is, even if the attorney can show that there is no substantial relationship between the subject of her representation of the current client and the subject of the lawsuit against the current client, it will still not save the attorney from disqualification. This is because an attorney has an obligation not only of confidentiality, but one of loyalty as well. The loyalty obligation arises out of the attorney's position as a fiduciary or trustee to the client. Therefore, in one of the few cases dealing with the subject, a federal appellate court held that in order to avoid disqualification, "the attorney must be prepared to show, at the very least, that there will be no actual or apparent conflict in loyalties or diminution in the vigor of his representation."[8]

If an attorney is disqualified from a particular representation because of a conflict of interests, can his associates or partners still continue the representation?

Absolutely not. The disqualification is carried over to all associates and partners of the attorney. In one recent case, the Minnesota Supreme Court stated the rule this way: "These rules [regarding conflicts of interest] apply to all members and associates of a law partnership regardless of whether the particular member later involved on behalf of a second client actually conferred with, and received information from, the first client."[9]

Can a law firm that has been disqualified from representing a client after it has started work on the client's behalf give its files to the successor counsel?

It depends. The courts seem willing, at least in complex cases, to allow the disqualified firm to give successor counsel its work product and related information, so long as no confidential information is included.[10]

If the associates and partners of a disqualified lawyer never received the confidential information he may have possessed, is the entire firm still disqualified?

Yes. The disqualification does not depend on the actual transfer of the information, only on the appearance of impropriety. Nor, under a recent 7th Circuit rule, can the firm escape disqualification by arguing conflicting interests are being represented by two different branches of the firm, which had constructed a "Chinese wall" between them.[11]

Does the same prohibition apply to lawyers who are not partners but simply share office space?

Several courts have held that it does and that if a lawyer is disqualified from accepting a certain representation, other lawyers who merely share office space with him are similarly disqualified.[12]

Can clients with conflicting interests agree to allow a single lawyer to represent both of them at the same time?

Yes, in some states, but there are circumstances in which even the clients may not agree. Here we are talking about simultaneous representation of conflicting interests. The rules are tougher than where the lawyer represents successive conflicting interests, the situation discussed earlier. In California, an attorney may represent litigants whose interests may conflict, providing the attorney makes a full disclosure and the litigants consent to the common representation. The consent may be express or implied.[13] On the other hand, other courts have ruled that there may be situations where the interests of the parties are

> so adverse and conflicting (or the possible collision or collusion between the interests can be so against public policy) that there could not properly be any dual representation even *with* and after full and complete disclosure and consent. In such a situation the court has inherent power to, and should, intervene to prevent it.[14]

The New York Court of Appeals has noted that representation of conflicting interests may be permissible in "exceptional situations," but even then "the lawyer, must, at the very least, disclose to all affected parties the nature and extent of the conflict and obtain their consent to the continued representation." In that particular case, the court ruled that it was unethical for a lawyer whose firm represented an insurance company to represent a claimant seeking payment from the insurance company at the same time. It did not matter that the insurance company was represented by one partner in the firm while the claimant was represented by another. The law firm did not reveal to the claimant that it also represented the insurance company. The court also emphasized that even in some cases where there is disclosure and consent, the conflict may be so "profound" that the dual representation will not be allowed. "This is true, for example, where the public interest is involved."[15]

Where might the public interest justify disqualifying an attorney from dual representation even if the clients knowingly consent?

Often in criminal cases. For example, in one New Jersey case, a lawyer represented a defendant charged with operating an illegal lottery. The lawyer's fee was paid by the defendant's employer. This situation created a conflict of interest which the defendant and his employer could not waive. On the one hand, it was to the advantage of the defendant to seek leniency by aiding the prosecutor by giving information about the employer. It was the duty of the attorney to so advise the defendant. On the other hand, since the attorney was being paid by the employer, he might have felt a loyalty to the people paying his fee not to encourage the defendant to cooperate with the authorities against them.[16]

In another case, involving certain "white-collar" crimes in connection with mortgage loans from the Federal Housing Administration, the same lawyer represented both the corporate defendant and an employee of the corporate defendant. The lawyer was paid by the corporation. The court held that this was improper since, on the one hand, the employee might wish to defend by asserting that she was doing what her corporate supervisors instructed, while, on the other hand, the corporation might wish to defend by claiming that the employee acted outside the instructions of her supervisors. The court ruled that "Choice of counsel should not be unnecessarily obstructed by the court . . . but where there is a serious possibility that a definite conflict of interest will arise, the necessities of sound judicial administration require the court to take command of the situation."[17]

Is it permissible for the same lawyer to represent two criminal defendants?

Yes, and it often happens. Multiple representation does not in and of itself violate the rights of the defendants or mean the lawyer is guilty of unethical behavior.[18] On the other hand, there can be conflicts of interest between defendants, and if so, joint representation can lead to a denial of the effective assistance of counsel.[19] In some jurisdictions, an indigent defendant is entitled to his own counsel, at least initially, to make sure there are no conflicts of interest. If it later seems that a joint representation will be best, the court can assign one counsel to represent more than one defendant.[20] In other jurisdictions, appointment of one counsel to represent more than one indigent defendant is acceptable so long as there is no real conflict of interests between the defendants.[21]

If a lawyer is representing more than one criminal defendant, whether appointed or retained to do so, it is her responsibility to bring the possibility of a conflict to the attention of the court as soon as she becomes aware of it.[22] Nevertheless, even if the lawyer fails in this responsibility, a conviction may be reversed if the joint representation amounts to a denial of the effective assistance of counsel under the Sixth Amendment.[23]

If a lawyer becomes aware that there is a conflict of interest in a multiple criminal representation, he will have to withdraw from representing one or possibly all of the clients, depending upon the nature of the confidential information he has acquired. For example, in one Kansas case, where a lawyer represented two defendants and learned that one of them was going to plead guilty and become a witness against the second, the lawyer was required to withdraw as the attorney for the second defendant. Furthermore, if he had already received information from the second defendant that could be used to assist in the plea negotiations of the defendant who wished to plead guilty, he would have been required to withdraw as counsel for both parties.[24]

Isn't there a danger that if the same lawyer represents a number of defendants in a criminal case they can more easily agree to lie or otherwise develop a strategy to defeat the prosecutor?

There is a danger that joint representation will be used for improper purposes, but this does not mean that it can be automatically disallowed. For example, in a recent case one attorney represented twenty-one union members subpoenaed to testify before a grand jury looking into the destruction of equipment at the *Washington Post*. Nineteen of the twenty-one witnesses invoked their privilege against self-incrimination. The United States attorney made a motion to disqualify the defense lawyer from representing all of the grand-jury witnesses. The court ruled that this motion was premature and that the appropriate remedy would be to have each of the witnesses brought before the district court, which could then inquire whether the privilege was being properly asserted.[25] On the other hand, other courts have been quicker to require separate counsel for grand-jury witnesses. Obviously, each case must be decided on its facts.[26]

We have been discussing representation of potentially conflicting interests in the context of litigation. Can an attorney represent two sides to a contract?

Yes. A distinction must be made between contracting parties whose interests coincide and contracting parties whose interests conflict. An attorney represents conflicting interests when "it becomes his duty, on behalf of one client, to contend for that which his duty to another client would require him to oppose."[27] When that happens, an attorney should cease to represent one or the other of the clients.[28] But so long as the two clients' interests coincide, there is no divided loyalty and no ethical problem. Nevertheless, the attorney must assume the "heavy burden" of assuring himself that there has been "full disclosure and full protection for both parties." If the interests of the two clients begin to conflict, it is best for the attorney to withdraw.[29]

Does this mean that a lawyer should never represent truly conflicting interests in a nonlitigation matter?

To be safe, she should not, although some courts have ruled that it is permissible if the clients know of the conflict and agree to the dual representation.[30] But this is sitting on a time bomb. If there is a dispute on the validity of the contract, the charge will almost certainly be made that the dual representation voids the agreement. So from the point of view of the lawyer—and the client who wants a binding contract—it is best to use two lawyers.

What about a lawyer who worked for the government and then goes into private practice? Is he limited in the clients he can represent?

Yes. As we saw, Disciplinary Rule 9-101(B) says that "A lawyer shall not accept private employment in a matter in which he had substantial responsibility while he was a public employee." Obviously, the key word is "substantial." Again, each case must be decided on its own facts. For example, in one case, an attorney worked for the Internal Revenue Service, representing it in connection with collection of certain income tax claims. The matter was settled. When the attorney left the government, he represented the taxpayers in a lawsuit by the government to foreclose tax liens based on the settlement. The attorney was disqualified. The court said that it was irrelevant whether the attorney had acquired any knowledge during his representation which could work to the disadvantage of the government in the foreclosure action.[31]

Sometimes the issue comes up in a completely different way. For example, in another case, an attorney worked for the United States Department of Justice, handling antitrust matters. In that capacity, he had "substantial responsibility" in bringing an antitrust claim against General Motors for monopolizing or attempting to monopolize the nationwide market for city and intercity buses. Later, he went to work for a private law firm. The City of New York, which was planning to file a complaint against General Motors for violation of the antitrust laws arising out of the same conduct the attorney had previously investigated while he was with the government, hired the attorney's new law firm "to assist in the preparation of the complaint." General Motors Corporation moved to disqualify the attorney from representing the city on the ground that the representation constituted "private employment in a matter in which he had substantial responsibility while he was a public employee."

The district judge declined to disqualify the attorney on the theory that the attorney "has not changed sides" (i.e., he was still representing the interests of a plaintiff) and that "there is nothing antithetical in the postures of the two governments in the actions in question." The Court of Appeals disagreed. It ruled that the ethical prohibition applies "irrespective of the side chosen in private practice." Furthermore, a contrary ruling raises the danger of a "great potential for lucrative returns in following into private practice the course already chartered with the aid of governmental resources."[32] It is noteworthy that in this case the attorney's prior employer, the United States government, was not objecting to his representation of the city. Rather, the defendant objected and its objection was upheld.

On the other hand, an attorney was not disqualified from representing former prisoners of war and other civilians in a private-securities fraud litigation because, while he was on temporary duty as a naval reserve attorney, he spent a few days investigating the same issue.[33]

What if a lawyer who worked for the government leaves and becomes a partner or associate in a firm that is handling a case substantially related to the nature of the lawyer's previous work for the government? Is the whole firm disqualified?

No. The court, in its discretion, can permit the firm to continue to conduct the litigation, but can require that there be appropriate "screening measures." These can include assuring that the former government employee has no connection with other firm members with regard to the subject matter of the case and has no access to the files on the case. One court has recently written that an inexorable disqualification of an entire firm for the disqualification of a single member or associate is entirely too harsh and should be mitigated by appropriate screening ... when truly unethical conduct has not taken place and the matter is merely one of the superficial appearance of evil, which a knowledge of the facts will dissipate. We note that the thousands of attorneys employed in Government do not, for the most part, have Civil Service protection, and are subject to removal without cause at any time. ... Should an attorney, having left Government perhaps contrary to his own volition, ineluctably infect all the members of any firm he joined with all his own personal disqualifications, he would take on the status of a Typhoid Mary, and be reduced to sole practice under the most unfavorable conditions.[84]

This rule with regard to former government lawyers is more liberal than the disqualification rules arising out of prior private representation. In the latter case, disqualification of one lawyer can, as we have seen, disqualify the entire firm. This is probably because a strict rule would work injustice given the pervasive character of government and the fact that the former government attorney will want to continue to work in the area in which he has developed expertise.

NOTES

1. *In re* Yarn Processing Patent Validity Litigation, 530 F.2d 83, 90 (5th Cir. 1976).
2. Erwin M. Jennings Co. v. Di Genova, 107 Conn. 491, 499, 141 A. 866, 868 (1928). *See also* Edelman v. Levy, 42 App. Div. 2d 758, 346 N.Y.S.2d 347 (2d Dept. 1973) ("An attorney must avoid not only the fact, but even the appearance, of representing conflicting interests.").
3. Gas-a-tron of Ariz. v. Union Oil Co. of Cal., 534 F.2d 1322 (9th Cir. 1976) *cert. denied,* 429 U.S. 861 (1976) (emphasis added).

4. Emle Industries, Inc. v. Patentex, Inc., 478 F.2d 562, 570–71 (2d Cir. 1973).

5. NCK Organization, Ltd. v. Bregman, 542 F.2d 128 (2d Cir. 1976).

6. International Elec. Corp. v. Flanzer, 527 F.2d 1288 (2d Cir. 1975). Allegaert v. Perot, 565 F.2d 246 (2d Cir. 1977).

7. Silver Chrysler-Plymouth, Inc. v. Chrysler Motors Corp., 518 F.2d 751 (2d Cir. 1975). *Cf.* Hull v. Celanese Corp., 513 F.2d 568 (2d Cir. 1975). *See also* Fred Weber, Inc. v. Shell Oil Co., 566 F.2d 602 (8th Cir. 1977) (refusal to disqualify plaintiff's civil antitrust lawyer who had previously represented codefendant in criminal antitrust case on ground that criminal case ended in no contest pleas and no substantive information had been provided.)

8. Cinema 5, Ltd. v. Cinerama, Inc., 528 F.2d 1384 (2d Cir. 1976).

9. Township Bd. of Lake Valley Twp. v. Lewis, 305 Minn. 488, 234 N.W.2d 815 (1975). *See also* Kurbitz v. Kurbitz, 77 Wash.2d 943, 468 P.2d 673 (1970). Cinema 5, *supra* note 8, at 1384, 1387.

10. First Wisconsin Mortgage Trust v. First Wisconsin Corp., 584 F.2d 201 (7th Cir. 1978) (*en banc*). International Business Machines Corp. v. Levin, 579 F.2d 271 (3rd Cir. 1978).

11. Schloetter v. Railoc of Ind., Inc., 546 F.2d 706 (7th Cir. 1976). *Cf.* American Can Co. v. Citrus Feed Co., 436 F.2d 1125 (5th Cir. 1971). Westinghouse Electric Corp. v. Kerr-McGee Corp., 580 F.2. 1311 (7th Cir. 1978), *cert. den.* —— U.S. —— (1978).

12. Kramer v. Scientific Control Corp., 534 F.2d 1085 (3d Cir. 1976) *cert. denied*, 429 U.S. 830 (1976) (holding that neither a member of the bar who is a plaintiff-class representative in a federal class action nor his officemate may serve as counsel for the class); *in re* Ridgely, 48 Del. 464, 106 A.D. 527 (1954). Zylstra v. Safeway Stores, Inc., 578 F.2d 102 (5th Cir. 1978) (same holding as Kramer, and further disqualifies spouse of disqualified attorney.)

13. Kagel v. First Commonwealth Co., 534 F.2d 194 (9th Cir. 1976).

14. Acorn Printing Co. v. Brown, 385 S.W.2d 812 (Mo. 1964) (emphasis in original).

15. Kelly v. Greason, 23 N.Y.2d 368, 376–78, 244 N.E.2d 456, 460–62, 296 N.Y.S.2d 937, 943–45 (1968).

16. *In re* Abrams, 56 N.J. 271, 266 A.2d 275 (1970).

17. United States v. Bernstein, 533 F.2d 775 (2d Cir. 1976), *cert. denied*, 429 U.S. 998 (1976).

THE RIGHTS OF LAWYERS AND CLIENTS

18. Collins v. Green, 505 F.2d 22 (5th Cir. 1974); Santoro v. United States, 462 F.2d 612 (9th Cir. 1972).
19. United States v. Marshall, 488 F.2d 1169 (9th Cir. 1973).
20. Ford v. United States, 379 F.2d 123 (D.C. Cir. 1967).
21. Foxworth v. Wainwright, 516 F.2d 1072 (5th Cir. 1975).
22. United States *ex rel.* Robinson v. Housewright, 525 F.2d 988 (7th Cir. 1975).
23. People v. Chacon, 69 Cal.2d 765, 447 P.2d 106 73 Cal. Rptr. 10 (1968). *See also* Annot., Circumstances Giving Rise to Conflict of Interest between or among Criminal Defendants Precluding Representation by Same Counsel, 34 A.L.R. 3d 470–507 (1970).
24. State v. Hilton, 217 Kan. 694, 538 P.2d 977 (1975).
25. *In re* Investigation before April 1975 Grand Jury, 531 F.2d 600 (D.C. Cir. 1976). *See also In re* Taylor, 567 F.2d 1183 (2nd Cir. 1977).
26. Pirillo v. Takiff, 341 A.2d 896, 462 Pa. 511 (1975), *cert. denied*, 423 U.S. 1083 (1976); *in re* Gopman, 531 F.2d 262 (5th Cir. 1976).
27. Florida Bar v. Moore, 194 So.2d 264, 269 (Fla. 1966).
28. *Ibid.*
29. Craft Builders, Inc. v. Ellis D. Taylor, Inc., ——Del. ——, 254 A.2d 233, 236 (1969).
30. *In re* Boivin, 271 Or. 419, 533 P.2d 171 (1975).
31. United States v. Trafficante, 328 F.2d 117 (5th Cir. 1964).
32. General Motors Corp. v. City of N.Y., 501 F.2d 639, 642, 650 (2d Cir. 1974).
33. Woods v. Covington County Bank, 537 F.2d 804 (5th Cir. 1976).
34. Kesselhaut v. United States, 555 F.2d 791, 793 (Ct. Cl. 1977). See also Opinion 889, Assoc. Bar City of N.Y., 31 REC. OF THE ASSOC. 552, 565 (Nov. 19, 1976); Formal Opinion 342, Comm. on Prof. Ethics, ABA.

VII

Attorneys' Fees and Attorneys' Liens

Who decides how much an attorney will be paid for taking a case?

The attorney and the client, as a rule. Generally, the size of an attorney's fee is determined by contract between the parties. If there is an express contract, oral or written, the amount of compensation it calls for is usually controlling.[1] On the other hand, if an attorney-client relationship arises but the parties do not agree on the amount of the attorney's fee, then the fee will be determined by the court (if the parties cannot agree between themselves) based on the reasonable value of the attorney's services.[2]

The only limitation on all this is that an attorney who undertakes to represent a client without discussing fee with the client in advance, cannot as a rule later decide that he was working on a contingent fee all along. A contingent fee, as we discuss below, is one that only becomes due if some specified event occurs—e.g., the client wins money. Since the lawyer working for a contingent fee takes a risk that the event may not occur and he will get no fee, contingent fees are usually higher than fees that are definite. If an attorney is free to wait until the specified event (or

117

contingency) is certain before choosing to work on a contingency fee, he will have the benefit of this higher fee without taking any of the risk.[3]

On the other hand, if an attorney does specify at the inception of the representation that he is working on a contingency but does not mention the amount or percentage of money he will receive if the contingency occurs, the court will award a reasonable sum.[4] Finally, an attorney and client may agree to a contingent fee after retainer but before the occurrence of the contingency, though the courts will carefully review such an agreement for fairness.[5]

Are contingent fees ever disallowed?

Yes. Contingent fees are not permitted in criminal actions. That is, a lawyer cannot agree with a criminal defendant that his fee or the size of his fee will depend on the verdict.[6] Contingent fees may also be disallowed in matrimonial actions. That is, a lawyer may not agree that his fee will depend on the size of the settlement or alimony he obtains for the wife in a divorce action.[7] Finally, even in actions where contingent fees are accepted, the fee may be disallowed if it results in an unconscionably high return to the lawyer.[8] There may be other situations in which a contingent fee may be disallowed as a matter of public policy or as contrary to ethical rules.[9]

If a client pays money to a lawyer as a retainer and then chooses not to proceed with the representation, can a client get the money back?

Generally, the client will not be able to get the money back unless there is an agreement between the attorney and the client that all or part of the retainer will be refunded if the client chooses not to go ahead with the litigation. There are limitations here, however. Clients have successfully sued for return of a portion of the retainer, though this is rare.[10] The courts retain residual power to review fee arrangements between lawyers and clients and to protect against unfairness.[11] Finally, there is the rarely invoked disciplinary rule prohibiting excessive fees. Conceivably, this rule can be used if to allow the lawyer to keep the full retainer would be shocking even to other lawyers.[12]

Are there any other cases in which a court will order an attorney to return a portion of the fee?

Yes, it does happen from time to time, but the lawbooks are not exactly full of such cases.[13] A client who wants to be careful should not pay his attorney a large fee in advance on the automatic assumption that he will get a portion of it back if the need for legal services disappears. The money will probably disappear too. Of course, if there is no question but that the lawyer's services will be needed, the problem does not arise. If the attorney insists on a substantial retainer in advance—which many attorneys will want—and there is a possibility that the case will terminate or "settle out" quickly, it is to the client's advantage to have the attorney put in writing the circumstances under which a portion of the fee will or may be returned.

Why is a contingent fee impermissible in domestic-relations cases?

The courts have never articulated a completely cogent reason. Apparently, they feel a contingent fee will encourage divorce and interfere with the maintenance of the family relation.[14] On the other hand, where an attorney was representing a deserted spouse not for the purpose of divorce or separation but to assist her in recovering her share of the assets of the marriage, a contingent fee was allowed.[15]

Exactly what is a contingent fee?

A contingent fee is a fee which becomes due to the lawyer only upon the happening of a specified contingency, usually recovery of money or success in the negotiation or litigation for which the lawyer has been retained. A fee can be *entirely* contingent, that is, the lawyer will get no fee at all if the contingency does not occur—unless, of course, the client makes the contingency impossible by dropping or settling the action or negotiation before it is concluded. In that case, the lawyer will be entitled to a reasonable fee for the services performed. A fee can also be *partially* contingent. This occurs, for example, where a lawyer charges a certain dollar amount plus (or against) a percentage of any recovery. So if a client has a possible $25,000 claim against a defendant, the lawyer may charge $2,000 plus one-fifth of any recovery. If the client recovers $25,000, the lawyer will get an additional $5,000 for a total fee of $7,000. If the client recovers less than $25,000, the lawyer will get one-fifth of the lesser amount. If the client recovers nothing, the lawyer only gets $2,000. In short, there are many ways to structure a fee arrangement between an attorney and a client. In the absence of fraud or overreaching, the fee arrangement the attorney and the client agree upon prior to the commencement of the representation will be enforced by the courts.[16]

What happens if a fee arrangement is not arrived at until after the attorney-client relationship has been established?

In those cases, the courts will be particularly careful in reviewing the arrangement to make sure that there has been no undue influence by the attorney on a client and that the client was fully informed before entering into the agreement.[17]

Is an attorney bound to follow minimum fee schedules set by local bar associations?

No. In fact, the United States Supreme Court has recently held that minimum fee schedules, at least those that were other than simply advisory, violated the antitrust laws of the United States and constituted illegal price-fixing. The court did not say how it would handle a "purely advisory fee schedule issued to provide guidelines, or an exchange of price information without a showing of an actual restraint on trade." But where a minimum fee schedule was "enforced through the prospective professional discipline from the State Bar, and a desire of attorneys to comply with announced professional norms," it was unlawful.[18]

Can a client ever get his opponent to pay his legal fees?

As a general rule, American law requires that each party to a litigation pay his or her own counsel fees. Even if a client wins, he will still have to pay his lawyer and cannot seek reimbursement from his losing adversary.[19]

There are only a few exceptions to this general rule. Some federal statutes, like the antitrust laws and some civil-rights laws, and some state statutes provide that a litigant who prevails in an action brought under the particular statute may also recover a reasonable attorney's fee from his opponent. A list of such federal statutes is in Appendix B. Second, two parties can agree that in the event of litigation between them, the prevailing party will have his attorney's fees paid by the losing party.[20]

Attorney's fees may be awarded by the court, even without statutory authority, if a party willfully violates a court order.[21] If a litigant brings an action in bad faith or for oppressive purposes, the court may also have authority to award attorney's fees to his opponent.[22] If a litigant sues on behalf of a number of people and creates a "common fund" in which they will all share, the court can award the litigant reasonable attorney's fees, to be paid out of that fund.[23] (We shall have more to say about this later.) Some states recognize a judicial power to award counsel fees in public-interest cases even if no "common fund" is created.[24]

What is an attorney's retainer?

Although "retainer" is generally used by attorneys to refer to the initial fee they expect to receive when the client hires them, it also refers to the scope of the attorney's authority. Thus, an attorney "retained" to bring an action against a landlord is authorized to act within the scope of that "retainer" or understanding. She is not authorized to act outside this scope. For example, she has no power to bind the client with respect to a dispute the client may be having with a debtor in a wholly unrelated situation. "Retainer" simply defines the scope of the attorney's authority to act for and bind the client.

The initial fee the attorney receives when she accepts the employment is also called a "retainer." It is not necessary, however, that there be an initial fee. An attorney can be retained in the sense that she becomes the client's agent for the purposes authorized, even though she has yet received no money. Indeed, as we have seen, an attorney-client relationship can arise even if the attorney provides her services gratis.

THE RIGHTS OF LAWYERS AND CLIENTS

When a court is required to determine the reasonable value of a lawyer's fee, what factors does it consider?

Many times this issue arises where an attorney has created a "common fund" for a group of plaintiffs and seeks his fee from it. In one case, the attorneys had succeeded in forcing the President of the United States to put a required pay raise into effect for millions of federal employees. The court held that the attorneys were entitled to a fee under the "common fund" exception to the general rule barring the award of attorneys' fees. This is how the appellate court instructed the lower court to make its determination of an appropriate fee:

> The inquiry begins with a determination of the time devoted to the litigation. This figure in turn is multiplied by an hourly rate for each attorney's work component, a rate which presumably would take into account the attorney's legal reputation and experience. The resulting figure represents an important starting point because it "provides the only objective basis for evaluating an attorney's services." In turn, this figure may be adjusted upward if there was a risk of non-compensation or partial compensation. In addition, the fees must be adjusted upward or downward on the basis of the quality of work performed as judged by the District Court.[25]

In another case, the attorneys brought a securities-fraud class action which resulted in a benefit to a class of shareholders in an amount exceeding $10,000,000. Subsequently, the attorneys who obtained this result applied for a counsel fee out of the fund. The court used the following factors in determining the appropriate compensation:

> The starting point is an evaluation of the attorneys' services in terms of time expended on the matter—an item deemed capable of objective determination based upon contemporaneous time records maintained by the attorneys. . . . After the time evaluation is made, then qualitative factors may be considered in deciding whether the compensation to be awarded should be increased or decreased. These factors include the risk

of litigation and of non-reimbursement of expenses in the event of non-recovery; the probability of success; the magnitude and complexity of the litigation; the responsibility undertaken; the expertise and standing of the attorneys who brought about the result; the strength of the opposition; the amount recovered; other results achieved and other factors.[26]

Of course, these cases involve large sums of money, not usually encountered in the average case in which a judge must determine a fee. The American Bar Association's Code of Professional Responsibility also lists several factors to consider in determining a reasonable fee. They are:

1. The time and labor required, the novelty and difficulty of the questions involved, and the skill requisite to perform the legal service properly.
2. The likelihood, if apparent to the client, that the acceptance of the particular employment will preclude other employment by the lawyer.
3. The fee customarily charged in the locality for similar legal services.
4. The amount involved and the results obtained.
5. The time limitations imposed by the client or by the circumstances.
6. The nature and length of the professional relationship with the client.
7. The experience, reputation, and ability of the lawyer or lawyers performing the services.
8. Whether the fee is fixed or contingent.[27]

Can the rule allowing lawyers to get counsel fees where they create a "common fund" or benefit for a class be used also in public-interest cases?

Sure, as long as a common fund is created. In fact, this is a major way in which public-interest litigation gets funded. In one recent case, the United States Court of Appeals for the Second Circuit affirmed an award in excess of $300,000 to a public-interest law firm in New York City which had successfully challenged the New York City Transit Authority's blanket policy of excluding from employment all persons participating in or having successfully concluded methadone maintenance programs.[28] In another case, public-interest lawyers successfully forced the government to release certain funds that had been appropriated by Congress for use by mental-health centers but which had been illegally impounded by the government. The court-awarded fee was $65,000.[29]

Is an attorney entitled to compensation for representing an indigent criminal defendant if there is no statute or court rule providing for compensation?

In most states the answer is no. An attorney can be required to represent an indigent criminal defendant without fee. Some courts see this as a lawyer's duty as an officer of the court, derived from her license to practice.[30] A few state courts, however, have ruled that an attorney appointed to represent an indigent has the right to be compensated at public expense.[31]

Can a lawyer participate in a system under which his clients can pay their fees through the use of bank credit cards?

Yes, in some states. New York, North Carolina, Texas, and Michigan are among the states that have accepted the use of credit cards to pay legal fees. Oregon and Arizona have accepted this system with some qualification. Florida and Illinois have rejected it. The New York Bar Association has approved the use of bank credit cards even where the bank charges interest on delinquent accounts.[32]

Can a lawyer give a fee to another lawyer who refers a case to him?

No. A fee for forwarding a case to another lawyer is unethical. A lawyer may not share in a fee unless he does work on the case and a division "is made in proportion to the services performed and responsibility assumed by each" lawyer.[33]

Is it an ethical violation for a lawyer to charge a client more than agreed for the same work?

Yes, and lawyers have been censured for such activity.[34]

ATTORNEYS' FEES AND ATTORNEYS' LIENS

Can a lawyer charge a client for out-of-pocket expenses connected with the representation?

Yes. The most obvious way this can happen is if the lawyer and the client agree that certain out-of-pocket expenses (e.g., photocopying, long-distance phone calls, travel, court costs) will be reimbursed by the client. But even without such an agreement, the client implicitly agrees that the attorney "is entitled to be reimbursed for such reasonable expenditures as the diligent prosecution or defense of the lawsuit may require." These disbursements do not include "expenditures which are a necessary part or adjunct of a properly equipped lawyer's office," such as secretarial time, local telephone costs, and the like.[35]

What if the attorney is discharged with cause? Is she entitled to a fee for the work done?

It depends on the jurisdiction. In some states, she is not and may even be required to repay any retainer.[36] Elsewhere, an attorney discharged with cause may still be entitled to obtain the reasonable value of her services rendered prior to the discharge.[37]

If a client discharges an attorney before the representation is completed, how is the value of his fee determined?

The court will usually determine the fee based on the reasonable value of the services provided by the attorney up until the time of his discharge. This is called *quantum meruit*, which means the value of the lawyer's work.[38] The rule may differ where the attorney is terminated under a "general retainer" (defined by time) rather than a "specific" one (defined by task). On a general retainer, the attorney may be entitled to the "value of the contract"—i.e., the amount of money he would have earned if he had been permitted to work for the full length of time contained in the agreement with the client—not just the value of the work already done.[39]

If an attorney is fired without cause, is the court, in determining the reasonable value of his services until the time of termination, limited to the amount agreed to between the attorney and the client?

No. The court can actually award more than the attorney and the client originally contemplated, even if the attorney is fired before he has completed all the work, so long as the termination is not with cause. Furthermore, the court can award compensation at a higher *rate* of pay than the original contract contemplated. This is because the court award is not based on the contract. Since the client breaches the contract by terminating the attorney—or, in states where this is not considered a breach, the client still subjects himself to pay the reasonable value of the attorney's services—the court is not bound by the contract.[40]

What if the attorney is discharged after completing her services?
The court can still award the attorney damages based on the reasonable value of her services, regardless of the contract amount. The lawyer is not limited to an action for the sum she would have been entitled to under the retainer.[41]

What happens if the attorney and the client agree that the attorney's fee will be contingent on their success in the lawsuit and then the client discharges the attorney, without cause, before the end of the lawsuit?
Any of three things can happen, depending upon the state in which the question arises. One possibility is that the attorney will be entitled to a fee only if the contingency eventually occurs.[42] In other jurisdictions, the attorney will be entitled only to the reasonable value of his services, whether or not the contingency occurs.[43] In yet other jurisdictions, the attorney will have the option of either accepting a fee for the reasonable value of his services, or of sticking with the contingency arrangement and taking a percentage of the recovery if there is one.[44]

What is an attorney's lien?
Actually there are two possible types of attorney's liens. Some states have both types, some only one, and some have neither; and the rules regarding each may differ from state to state.

One type of lien is called a "retaining lien." In most states that recognize this lien, it rests on common law, that is, the lien exists as a result of rules created by the courts themselves.[45] In some states, the legislature has defined the retaining lien by statute and the statute has been interpreted to replace the common law, assuming that the state recognized the retaining lien in common law to begin with.[46] In those states which do recognize a retaining lien as a matter of common law, the lien is upon the "clients' papers actually in [the attorney's] possession which entitles him to retain the papers until his claim for services is paid . . . or until it is determined that he is not due any money or that he has been guilty of unprofessional conduct."[47] In other words, a retaining lien gives the lawyer the right to keep the papers and property of the client in his actual possession until he has been paid.[48] It is important to emphasize that the property must be in the attorney's actual possession. If an attorney returns property to a client, he cannot later assert a lien on that property.[49]

The other kind of lien is called a "charging lien." Some state courts have considered this lien also to have existed at common law, while other courts have ruled that the charging lien is a statutory lien only. Most states recognize the charging lien. The charging lien gives the attorney an interest in the client's cause of action or claim. The lien "attaches," that is, it becomes enforceable, when the client obtains a judgment or verdict for money or something of value. The lien attaches to the subject matter of the judgment. Furthermore, the lien *follows* the subject matter of the judgment. This means that if the client transfers the person has an obligation to the lawyer to pay him out of the judgment. In addition, the client cannot in any way defeat the charging lien by settling his claim. In order to enforce the lien, or to determine its scope, the attorney, or the client, can ask the court to rule.[50]

At common law, the charging lien was narrower than this description, which is based on the New York statute. At common law, the charging lien did not arise *until* there was actually a judgment or verdict in favor of the client. Under the New York statute and statutes in other states, the charging lien applies to the cause of action or claim of the client even before it results in a judgment, although, obviously, it cannot be enforced until a judgment produces money or other thing of value against which the lien can operate.[51]

It is not necessary, in order to have a charging lien, that the attorney possess anything at all of the client's. This is how a charging lien differs from a retaining lien.[52] On the other hand, it is not possible to have a charging lien unless the attorney is acting in an affirmative, rather than a defensive, capacity for the client—that is, the attorney must be representing a plaintiff (or a defendant who asserts a counterclaim), since the charging lien depends on the existence of a judgment for something of value before it can operate. If an attorney is simply representing a defendant who does not have an affirmative claim, nothing of value will be created and there is nothing for the charging lien to attach to.[53] The retaining lien, on the other hand, exists so long as the attorney has property of the client in his possession. It does not depend on the creation of a fund through a judgment for something of value.[54]

If a lawyer is holding money for a client in trust, can she enforce her lien by deducting the amount of her fee from the trust money and put it in her own account?

No. A lawyer may not unilaterally determine her fee and take it out of trust money.[55]

Is there any property upon which a lien may not operate?

Yes, public policy excludes certain property from the operation of either lien. For example, child-support payments are not subject to an attorney's lien.[56] Likewise, alimony is immune.[57] Where an attorney receives funds for a specific purpose, to which he agrees to apply the funds, the lien will not attach to those funds, but the attorney must carry out the agreed purpose.[58]

Does an attorney's lien arise even where he is retained on a contingent basis?

Absolutely, although his right to a fee depends on the occurrence of the contingency. But if the contingency occurs, both a charging and retaining lien can be used to protect the attorney, and the retaining lien can be used while the attorney is waiting for the contingency to occur.

Furthermore, it is no defense to the attorney's use of these liens that the underlying claim was never litigated to judgment because the parties may have stipulated for a settlement of a certain amount. The lien attaches to the settlement.[59]

Can an attorney and a client agree at the outset of the representation that the attorney will assert no liens or have liens not otherwise recognized?

Absolutely. Where the lien is recognized as a matter of common law or statutory law, it exists to protect the attorney. The attorney can agree to waive, completely or partly, the protection afforded.[60] Conversely, where a state does not recognize an attorney's lien, the client can agree in the contract with the attorney that the attorney will have either a retaining or charging lien or both.[61]

How does a lawyer enforce his retaining or charging liens?

An attorney enforces a charging lien by bringing a legal action or proceeding to have the amount of his fee determined (if it is not already clear) and to obtain a court order awarding him that amount out of the fund or judgment created. The retaining lien, however, is not enforced by bringing an action for the attorney's fee based on the lien. Such an action may, of course, be brought independently of the lien, but that is no different from the right of any creditor to sue any debtor for the value of his services. The retaining lien is "enforced" in another way. The lawyer simply keeps the client's papers, including such things as stock certificates, deeds, bankbooks, cash, and other valuable papers, until the client pays him. It is like a stalemate. The papers and documents may not be useful to the lawyer, but neither will the client get any use out of them until the lawyer is paid. If and when the lawyer is paid, the papers and documents must be returned.[62]

What if the client needs the papers and documents for the continuation of the litigation?

The court does have it within its power to order the attorney to deliver any documents in his possession, although the court will make provision for protection of the attorney. An attorney who obeys such an order does not waive his retaining lien.[63]

What if the client goes bankrupt before he has paid his lawyer and while the lawyer's retaining lien is in existence?

An attorney's retaining lien survives the bankruptcy of her client. "The attorney simply has the right to hold the client's papers until the legal fees are paid. This right is enforceable against the client ... and the trustee in bankruptcy."[64]

Can a lawyer advance the court costs and other expenses of litigation for a client with no money?

Only if the client is obligated to repay the money, whether or not the lawyer wins the case. Otherwise the lawyer may be guilty of "maintenance," i.e., supporting a litigation. This rule also applies to funds advanced to permit the client to live while the case is in progress.[65] The long-standing prohibition against maintenance may be in line for some qualification as a result of possible changes in the solicitation rules. See Chapter IX.

NOTES

1. N.Y. Jud. Law §474 (McKinney); Rodkison v. Haecker, 248 N.Y. 480, 162 N.E. 493 (1928); Anderson's Estate v. Smith, ——Ind. App. ——, 316 N.E.2d 592 (1974).
2. Trafton v. Youngblood, 69 Cal.2d 17, 442 P.2d 648, 69 Cal. Rptr. 568 (1968).
3. *See* cases discussed in DeGraff v. McKesson & Robbins, Inc., 31 N.Y.2d 862, 869–72, 292 N.E.2d 310, 340 N.Y.S.2d 171, 178–79 (1972) (Breitel, dissenting.)
4. Degraff v. McKesson & Robbins, Inc., 31 N.Y.2d 862, 292 N.E.2d 310, 340 N.Y.S.2d 171 (1972).
5. Rock v. Ballou, 286 N.C. 99, 209 S.E.2d 476 (1974).
6. Peyton v. Margiotti, 398 Pa. 86, 90, 156 A.2d 865, 867 (1959).
7. Levine v. Levine, 206 Misc. 884, 135 N.Y.S.2d 304 (Sup. Ct. Queens County 1954); *in re* Brackett, 114 App. Div.

257, 99 N.Y.S. 802 (3d Dept 1906), aff'd, 189 N.Y. 502, 81 N.E. 1160 (1907).
8. McCreary v. Joel, 186 So.2d 4 (Fla. 1966); Florida Bar v. Moriber, 314 So.2d 145 (Fla. 1975) (improper to use contingent fee in case presenting no difficulty and which could easily have been handled by a layman); *in re* Gasco, 27 A.D.2d 557, 275 N.Y.S.2d 871 (2d Dept. 1966).
9. Melendres v. City of Los Angeles, 45 Cal. App. 3d 267, 119 Cal. Rptr. 713 (1975); William Mayer, Jr., Co., v. Union Parts Mfg. Co., 188 Misc. 383, 67 N.Y.S.2d 885 (Sup. Ct. N.Y. County 1946) (contingent fee dependent upon the procurement of a government contract by a specific agent would be void).
10. Greene v. McIntyre, 119 Ga. App. 296, 167 S.E.2d 203 (1969). *But see* Fellner v. Zuckerberg, 202 Misc. 611, 118 N.Y.S.2d 470 (App. T. 1st Dept. 1952) (where entire fee paid before client decided not to go ahead with annulment, return of funds dependent upon intent of the parties).
11. Farmington Dowel Prod. Co. v. Forster Mfg. Co., 421 F.2d 61 (1st Cir. 1970); Cohen v. Ryan, 34 App. Div. 2d 789, 311 N.Y.S.2d 644 (2d Dept. 1970).
12. Disciplinary Rule 2-106(A) and (B), Code of Professional Responsibility, ABA.
13. McInerney v. Massasoit Greyhound Ass'n, 359 Mass. 339, 269 N.E.2d 211 (1971); *in re* Cohen, 169 App. Div. 544, 155 N.Y.S. 517 (1st Dept. 1915); Wade v. Clemmons, 84 Misc. 2d 822, 377 N.Y.S.2d 415 (Sup. Ct. Kings County 1975). *Cf.* Taraborrelli v. Vinciguerra, 27 App. Div. 2d 749, 277 N.Y.S.2d 468 (2d Dept. 1967).
14. Avant v. Whitten, 253 So.2d 394 (Miss. 1971); Sobieski v. Maresco, 143 So.2d 62 (Fla. Dist. Ct. App. 1962); Barelli v. Levin, 144 Ind. App. 576, 247 N.E.2d 847 (1969); McDearmon v. Gordon & Gremillion, 247 Ark. 318, 445 S.W.2d 488 (1969).
15. Burns v. Stewart, 290 Minn. 289, 188 N.W.2d 760 (1971).
16. Burns v. Valene, 298 Minn. 257, 214 N.W.2d 686 (1974); Herro, McAndrews and Porter, S.C. v. Gerhardt, 62 Wis. 2d 179, 214 N.W.2d 401 (1974).
17. Randolph v. Schuyler, 284 N.C. 496, 201 S.E.2d 833 (1974); *in re* Vaupel's Estate, 266 App. Div. 723, 40 N.Y.S.2d 956 (1st Dept. 1943).
18. Goldfarb v. Virginia State Bar, 421 U.S. 773, 781 (1975).
19. Alyeska Pipeline Service Co. v. Wilderness Society, 421 U.S. 240 (1975).
20. 379 Madison Ave., Inc. v. Stuyvesant Co., 242 App. Div. 567, 275 N.W.S. 953 (1st Dept. 1934), aff'd, 268 N.Y. 576, 198 N.E. 412 (1935).

21. Toledo Scale Co. v. Computing Scale Co., 261 U.S. 399, 426–28 (1923).
22. Vaughan v. Atkinson, 369 U.S. 527, 530–31 (1962).
23. Mills v. Electric Auto-Lite Co., 396 U.S. 375, 391–92 (1970).
24. Serrano v. Priest, 20 Cal.3d 25, 569 P.2d 1303, 141 Cal. Rptr. 315 (1977).
25. National Treasury Employees Union v. Nixon, 521 F.2d 317, 322 (D.C. Cir. 1975).
26. Blank v. Talley Indus., Inc., 390 F. Supp. 1, 3 (S.D.N.Y. 1975). *See also* Dorey Corp. v. E.I. duPont de Nemours & Co., 426 F. Supp. 944 (S.D.N.Y. 1977); City of Detroit v. Grinnell Corp., 495 F.2d 448, 468 (2d Cir. 1974); Lindy Bros. Bldrs. v. American Radiator & Standard Corp., 487 F.2d 161, 169–70 (3d Cir. 1973); Vincent v. Hughes Air West, Inc., 557 F.2d 759 (9th Cir. 1977); Prandini v. National Tea Co., 557 F.2d 1015 (3d Cir. 1977). *See also* City of Detroit v. Grinnell Corp., 560 F.2d 1093 (2d Cir. 1977) (Grinnell II) for a discussion of subtleties in this area.
27. Disciplinary Rule 2-106(D) (1)-(8), Code of Professional Responsibility, ABA.
28. Beazer v. New York City Transit Auth. 558 F.2d 97 (2d Cir. 1977), *cert. granted*, —— U.S. —— (1978).
29. National Council of Community Health Centers v. Mathews, 546 F.2d 1003 (D.C. Cir. 1977), *cert. denied*, —— U.S. —— (June 6, 1977).
30. Young v. State, 255 So.2d 318 (Miss. 1971).
31. Luke v. County of Los Angeles, 269 Cal.App.2d 495, 74 Cal. Rptr. 771 (1969); State v. Green, 470 S.W.2d 571 (Mo. 1971); Bradshaw v. Ball, 487 S.W.2d 294 (Ky. 1972). Other states taking this position include Indiana, Iowa, Nebraska, New Jersey, and Wisconsin.
32. Opinion 362, New York State Bar Ass'n (1974); Opinion 399, NYSBA (1975); Opinion 338, ABA (1974).
33. Disciplinary Rule 2-107(A)(2), Code of Professional Responsibility, ABA; Ethical Consideration 2-22, Code of Professional Responsibility, ABA; Palmer v. Breyfogle, 217 Kan. 128, 535 P.2d 955 (1975).
34. *In re* Karp, 240 App. Div. 388, 270 N.Y.S. 113 (1st Dept. 1934), *aff'd*, 266 N.Y. 473, 195 N.E. 160, 278 N.Y.S. Appdx. (1934); *in re* Nevins, 285 App. Div. 202, 135 N.Y.S.2d 604 (1st Dept. 1954).
35. Rao v. Noferi, 50 Misc. 2d 60, 269 N.Y.S.2d 534 (App. T. 1st Dept. 1966).
36. Coclin Tobacco Co. v. Griswold, 408 F.2d 1338 (1st Cir.

1969), *cert. denied*, 396 U.S. 940 (1969); First Nat'l Bank of Cincinnati v. Pepper, 454 F.2d 626 (2d Cir. 1972).
37. Fracasse v. Brent, 6 Cal.3d 784, 494 P.2d 9, 100 Cal. Rptr. 385 (1972).
38. Bradbury v. Farber, 31 App. Div. 2d 824, 298 N.Y.S.2d 29 (2d Dept. 1969); Leighton v. New York, Susquehanna & W. R.R., 303 F. Supp. 599 (S.D.N.Y. 1969), *aff'd*., 455 F.2d 389 (2d Cir. 1972), *cert. denied*, 406 U.S. 920 (1972); Paolillo v. American Export Isbrandtsen Lines, Inc., 305 F. Supp. 250 (S.D.N.Y. 1969).
39. Prial v. Supreme Court Uniformed Officers Ass'n, 89 Misc. 2d 287, 397 N.Y.S.2d 528 (Sup. Ct. App. T. 1st Dept. 1977).
40. Hill v. Severn, 23 App. Div. 2d 902, 258 N.Y.S.2d 857 (3d Dept. 1965).
41. Kronish, Lieb, Shainswit, Weiner & Hellman v. Howard Stores Corp., 44 App. Div. 813, 355 N.Y.S.2d 426 (1st Dept. 1974).
42. Fracasse, *supra* note 37.
43. Krebs v. Bailey's Equipment Rentals, Inc., 328 So.2d 775 (La. App. 1976); Dill v. Public Util. Dist. No. 2, 3 Wash. App. 360, 475 P.2d 309 (1970). *Cf*. People v. Radinsky, 182 Colo. 259, 512 P.2d 627 (1973).
44. Paolillo, *supra* note 38; Burns, *supra* note 15.
45. *In re* Heinsheimer, 214 N.Y. 361, 108 N.E. 636 (1915).
46. Akers v. Akers, 233 Minn. 133, 46 N.W.2d 87 (1951); Academy of Cal. Optometrists, Inc. v. Superior Court for Sacramento County, 51 Cal. App. 3d 999, 124 Cal. Rptr. 668 (1975).
47. Mongitore v. Murphy, 42 App. Div. 2d 800, 346 N.Y.S.2d 420 (3d Dept. 1973); *in re* Weitling, 266 N.Y. 184, 194 N.E. 401 (1935).
48. *In re* Browy, 527 F.2d 799 (7th Cir. 1976) (retaining lien enforceable against third parties).
49. Goldman v. Rafel Estates, Inc., 269 App. Div. 647, 58 N.Y.S.2d 168 (1st Dept. 1945).
50. N.Y. JUD LAW §475 (McKinney); United States v. Transocean Air Lines, Inc., 386 F.2d 79 (5th Cir. 1967), *cert. denied*, 389 U.S. 1047 (1968).
51. Randall v. Van Wagenen, 115 N.Y. 527, 22 N.E. 361 (1889). For an example of a fairly narrow charging lien, *see* United States v. Fidelity Philadelphia Trust Co., 459 F.2d 771 (3rd Cir. 1972) (Pennsylvania law).
52. Forrest Currell Lumber Co. v. Thomas, 82 N.M. 789, 487 P.2d 491 (1971).
53. Torphy v. Reder, 357 Mass. 153, 257 N.E.2d 435 (1970); Morateck v. Milwaukee Auto Mut. Ins. Co., 34 Wis.2d

95, 148 N.W.2d 704 (1967); Spinello v. Spinello, 70 Misc. 2d 521, 334 N.Y.S.2d 70 (Sup. Ct. Nassau County 1972).
54. *In re* Cooper, 291 N.Y. 254, 52 N.E.2d 421 (1943).
55. Greenbaum v. State Bar of Cal., 15 Cal.3d 893, 544 P.2d 921, 126 Cal. Rptr. 785 (1976).
56. Fuqua v. Fuqua, 88 Wash.2d 100, 558 P.2d 801 (1977).
57. Owen v. Forchelli, 42 Misc. 2d 1064, 249 N.Y.S.2d 913 (Sup. Ct. N.Y. County 1964).
58. Marsano v. State Bank of Albany, 27 App. Div. 2d 411, 279 N.Y.S.2d 817 (3d Dept. 1967); Entertainment and Amusements of Ohio, Inc. v. Barnes, 49 Misc. 2d 316, 267 N.Y.S.2d 359 (Sup. Ct. Onondaga County 1966).
59. United States v. Transocean Air Lines, Inc., 356 F.2d 702 (5th Cir. 1966).
60. Gross v. Holzworth, 151 Mont. 179, 440 P.2d 765 (1968).
61. Weiss v. Marcus, 51 Cal. App. 3d 590, 124 Cal. Rptr. 297 (1975). *Cf. in re* Loring, 62 N.J. 336, 301 A.2d 721 (1973).
62. Midvale Motors Co. v. Saunders, 21 Utah 2d 181, 442 P.2d 938 (1968); *in re* Weitling, *supra* note 47.
63. Goldenstein v. Goldenstein, 28 App. Div. 2d 962, 283 N.Y.S.2d 167 (1st Dept. 1967); City of Hankinson v. Otter Tail Power Co., 294 F. Supp. 249 (D.N.D. 1969); People v. Altvater, 78 Misc. 2d 24, 355 N.Y.S.2d 736 (Sup. Ct. Bronx County 1974).
64. *In re* Browy, 527 F.2d 799, 801 (7th Cir. 1976).
65. Mahoning County Bar Ass'n v. Ruffalo, 179 Ohio St. 263, 199 N.E.2d 396, *cert. denied* 379 U.S. 931 (1964); *see also* Annot. 8 A.L.R. 2d 1155 (1966).

VIII

Malpractice and Deals Between Attorney and Client

What is legal malpractice?

Legal malpractice consists of the failure of an attorney "to use such skill, prudence, and diligence as lawyers of ordinary skill and capacity commonly possess and exercise in the performance of the tasks which they undertake." . . . When such failure proximately [or substantially] causes damage, it gives rise to [i.e., gives the client] an action in tort. Since in the usual case, the attorney undertakes to perform his duties pursuant to a contract with the client, the attorney's failure to exercise the requisite skill and care is also a breach of an express or implied term of that contract. Thus, legal malpractice generally constitutes both a tort and a breach of contract.[1]

What if the lawyer also violates her ethical responsibilities? Can this be legal malpractice as well?

Yes. If a lawyer breaches a confidence of a client, or represents conflicting interests, or steals a client's money or violates any other of the ethical provisions she is required to follow for the protection of the client, she will also be guilty of legal malpractice and have to pay the client damages for any loss the client may suffer.[2]

How much skill does an attorney have to exercise in representing a client?

Different courts answer this question in slightly different ways. A review of several cases will give you a sense of the required level of competence. In one case, the attorney for a defendant convicted of murder submitted a four-page brief to the appeal court and did not ask for oral argument. The court, while affirming the conviction because guilt was clear, took the occasion to remind the bar "that lawyers owe their clients obligations of competence, diligence, and zeal, and that those obligations may comprehend, upon appeal, both the presentation of the law and the marshalling of the facts."[3]

In another famous case, a lawyer representing a woman in a divorce action failed to include, on the list of community property in which she claimed a share, her husband's sizable military pension. When this failure was discovered, it was too late to change the decree, with the result that the woman lost substantial sums in alimony and child support. The California Supreme Court affirmed a malpractice judgment against the woman's lawyer. The lawyer had argued that the law was unclear and that he should not be responsible for mistaken advice when well-informed lawyers in the community entertain reasonable doubt about the proper resolution of the particular question involved. The court rejected this argument. The lawyer should have known that the military pension was part of the community property in which the wife had an interest. The court said that

> the crucial inquiry is whether [the lawyer's] advice was so legally deficient when it was given that he may be found to have failed to use "such skill, prudence and diligence as lawyers of ordinary skill and capacity commonly possess and exercise in the performance of the tasks which they undertake."

The court went on and said that a lawyer is expected

to possess knowledge of those plain and elementary principles of law which are commonly known by well-informed attorneys, and to discover those additional rules of law which, although not commonly known, may readily be found by standard research techniques. . . . If the law on a particular subject is doubtful or debatable, an attorney will not be held responsible for failing to anticipate the manner in which the uncertainty will be resolved. . . . But even with respect to an unsettled area of the law, we believe an attorney assumes an obligation to his client to undertake reasonable research in an effort to ascertain relevant legal principles and to make an informed decision as to a course of conduct based upon an intelligent assessment of the problem.[4]

In yet another case, a client made a $250,000 loan after his attorney negligently failed to provide him with material information with regard to the risk involved. The client sued the attorney and prevailed.[5] Finally, in another case, the attorney failed to start the client's lawsuit before the statute of limitations on the action ran out. The client sued and won a judgment of $81,250 against the attorney.[6]

Can a lawyer be wrong without being liable to her client for malpractice?

Yes. A lawyer does not guarantee, when she gives advice, that her opinion or analysis of the law will be infallible. If the attorney exercises an informed judgment, she will not be liable for malpractice even if it turns out that she was wrong.[7] This is a question of degree. To equal malpractice, the attorney must act in a way that shows she lacks the customary knowledge and skill possessed by members of the profession in the state where she practices.[8]

Is a lawyer liable to a client for malpractice even though the client suffers no damage?

No. This is not like a disciplinary proceeding where a lawyer may be disciplined, even disbarred, although his unethical conduct has caused no harm. This is a civil action based on tort or contract. As in other civil actions, in order to prevail, the client must show that he has been damaged as a result of the attorney's failure to exercise required care. In other words, the client must have a loss proximately caused by the attorney's conduct.[9] The attorney is liable to the client only for those responsibilities that are within the confines of the attorney-client retainer.[10]

Is an attorney's law firm responsible for the attorney's malpractice?

Yes. A law firm, as well as each lawyer in it, is generally responsible for the malpractice of its partners and associates.[11] On the other hand, in some states, if a law firm practices as a professional association or professional corporation, and not as a partnership, while the corporation may be liable for the negligence of all of its lawyer employees, the individual stockholder-owners (attorneys) will be personally liable only for their own negligence and the negligence of those they supervise.[12]

If an attorney's malpractice causes a client a loss, but the client is jointly negligent in bringing about the loss, will this defeat or reduce recovery?

Some cases have held that contributory negligence by the client will either reduce or defeat recovery for loss from an attorney's malpractice.[13]

Can a criminal defendant who is convicted sue her lawyer for malpractice?

Yes. If the conviction resulted from the lawyer's negligence, the defendant can sue for malpractice. The defendant will have to prove that the attorney's negligence was the proximate cause of the defendant's loss—in this case, the loss is the fine, the jail sentence, or the fact that the defendant has a criminal conviction. These cases are rare, and success in them is even more rare.[14]

Can an attorney ever be liable for malpractice to persons other than his immediate client?

Yes. This is a new and expanding area of the law. The circumstances under which attorneys can be liable to third persons as a result of their negligence or willful misconduct are not yet clearly defined. In one recent case, a man and his former wife agreed that the temporary custody of their infant daughter would be transferred to the former wife for several weeks in the summer. Since the former wife was Swiss, the court entered an order, to which the parties agreed, that the former wife's attorney would deliver the passports for the mother and the child to a neutral lawyer, who would hold them until the period of visitation was completed. The child was transferred to the mother, but her lawyer did not deliver the passports as required. Instead, he gave them to the mother, who proceeded to take the child out of the country. The father sued the wife's attorney for malpractice and sought damages for the mental anguish arising out of the lost contact with his child. The Supreme Court of Oregon held that these facts justified an award of damages against the wife's attorney.[15]

In another case, an attorney gave his clients legal advice that they could issue certain shares of stock to themselves as dividends without endangering the exemption of this stock from certain registration requirements. The clients followed the advice, issued the stock, and then sold the stock to certain purchasers. The attorney's advice was incorrect, and, as a result of the activity, the SEC suspended the exemption from registration, with consequent loss in the value of the stock. The purchasers sued the attorney. The court held that the attorney had no relationship to the purchasers that

> would give rise to his owing [the purchasers] any duty of care in advising his clients that they could sell the stock without adverse consequences. . . . To make an attorney liable for negligent confidential advice not only to the client who enters into a transaction in reliance upon the advice but also to the other parties to the transaction with whom the client deals at arm's length would inject undesirable self-protective reservations into the attorney's counseling role. The attorney's preoccupation or concern with the possibility of claims based on mere negligence (as distinct from fraud or malice) by any with whom his client might deal "would prevent him from devoting his entire energies to his client's interests."[16]

Where an attorney fails to draft a will as directed by his client, or drafts it incompetently, so that certain intended beneficiaries lose their inheritance, the California Supreme Court has held that the attorney will be liable to the beneficiaries for their loss.[17] On the other hand, New York courts have held just the opposite.[18]

The Oregon Supreme Court has ruled that an attorney who knowingly participates or aids in the sale of unregistered securities will be liable to purchasers, even though they may not be his clients. He will not be liable, however, if his only action is to prepare documents relating to the securities without knowledge of their lack of registration.[19]

Finally, in a California case, a creditor gave the responsibility to collect his loan to a collection agency. The agency employed an attorney, who brought an action but then failed to prosecute it diligently. The creditor sued the attorney directly. The California court held that this was a valid claim, even though the creditor was not the client of the attorney.[20]

Is there a trend toward increasing the responsibility of attorneys for the losses of third parties resulting from the attorneys' negligence?

Definitely, although the trend is slow in developing momentum.[21] On the other hand, some courts, in New York and elsewhere, continue to adhere to the more conservative position that attorneys are not liable for a loss to third persons resulting from their negligence if the acts of the attorneys were "performed in good faith and for the honest purpose of protecting the interests of their clients." New York continues to require a showing that the attorney has been "guilty of fraud or collusion, or of a malicious or tortious act."[22]

If an attorney commits malpractice, how long does the client have in order to sue?

In different states, the period of the statute of limitations will differ. In New York, for example, it is three years.[23] In California it is two years.[24] The more interesting question is when the statute of limitations *begins* to run. If it begins to run from the time that the malpractice is committed, whether or not the client knows or should reasonably know of it, it may run out before the client ever becomes aware that malpractice occurred. For this reason, several states have adopted a more enlightened rule under which the limitation period does not begin to run until the client discovers, or in the exercise of reasonable diligence should have discovered, the facts which give rise to the cause of action.[25]

Can a client, in addition to suing for malpractice, begin a disciplinary proceeding against a lawyer?

No. Only duly appointed grievance or bar-association committees can do this. A private person can, of course, complain to such a committee, but she cannot begin a disciplinary action.[26]

Can an attorney who represents a client at the same time have an interest that is in opposition to her client's interests?

No, and it doesn't matter how benevolent the attorney's motives are or that she was in complete good faith in doing so. In one recent California Supreme Court case, attorneys acquired a first deed of trust on certain real property at a time when their clients held a promissory note secured by a second deed of trust on the same property. The attorneys eventually foreclosed their first deed, thereby becoming owners of the property. The attorneys contended, and in fact the disciplinary board agreed, that they purchased the first deed of trust in order to give their clients time to raise sufficient money to protect their interests in the property. It was also found that the attorneys were acting in what they considered to be the best interests of their clients and had no intent to deceive or defraud them. Furthermore, the purchase of the first deed of trust was done with the knowledge and consent of the clients. After the clients were unable to raise sufficient funds to buy the property from the attorneys, the attorneys foreclosed on the property and purchased it themselves.

The California Supreme Court concluded that this was a violation justifying a private reprimand. While the court's decision depended on a particular rule of the California Rules of Professional Conduct prohibiting a lawyer from acquiring "an interest adverse to his client," it is likely that the same result would be reached in other jurisdictions. While the rule did not prohibit every business transaction engaged in by an attorney with his client, it did prohibit acquisition of an "adverse" interest. The existence of two deeds of trust on the same property, with other factors in the case, made the attorneys' interest adverse to that of their clients.[27]

Can a lawyer and his client enter into business deals together if the lawyer's interest is not adverse to the client?

Yes, but the lawyer has to be very, very careful. Business deals between a lawyer and a client entered into after the creation of the attorney-client relationship will be viewed with suspicion and closely scrutinized for unfairness or overreaching.[28] The lawyer must fully disclose the facts of the transaction, its legal consequences, and the respective obligations and rights of each of the parties.[29] In some states, the attorney-client business deal is even presumptively invalid and the presumption can be overcome only by the clearest and most convincing evidence showing full and complete disclosure of all the facts known to the attorney, with total independence of action by the client.[30] The agreement will be construed by the courts most favorably to the client.[31] In some states, where an attorney changes the fee arrangement with the client after the attorney-client relationship has already been formed, the new fee arrangement will be presumed to be fraudulent unless the attorney can affirmatively prove that the modification was made in good faith, free from undue influence, and with adequate consideration.[32]

What if the client is worldly and experienced in business matters?

This will make no difference if the attorney did not make a full disclosure of the client's rights and liabilities under the agreement between them or did not provide the client with advice which he would have given if the client had been dealing with a third person.[33]

Can a client give an attorney a gift?

Yes, if it is given freely and voluntarily and without any imposition by the attorney. But a court can set aside a gift

142

if it concludes that it was given through undue influence of the attorney upon the client.[34]

What are an attorney's obligations if he receives funds on behalf of a client?

He must notify the client immediately and pay over the money, except to the extent that the client and the attorney have an understanding otherwise. Since these are not trust funds or funds which the attorney has previously agreed to use only for a limited purpose, he may deduct his fees and disbursements before paying the balance. The attorney must give his client a complete accounting, that is, an explanation of how much money he holds in his possession for the client, where it came from, why it is in the amount that it is, and, if there were deductions, the reasons for the deductions.[35]

Must an attorney keep her clients' funds in a separate account?

She should, and in some states she can be disciplined for failure to do so, even though she never actually uses clients' money for her own purposes. An attorney should never "commingle" a client's funds with her own.[36]

Can a client leave property to the attorney who drafts his will?

Yes. A client is legally competent to make his attorney a beneficiary under his will, but, depending upon the facts and circumstances involved, the courts may conclude that there was undue influence in causing the client to leave the attorney an inheritance. Among the factors considered by the courts are whether the attorney participated in the preparation or execution of the will, the size of the gift, the client's physical and mental condition, and whether the client had independent advice.[37]

NOTES

1. Neel v. Magana, Olney, Levy, Cathcart & Gelfand, 6 Cal.3d 837, 98 Cal. Rptr. 837 491 P.2d 421, (1971).

2. *See, e.g.*, Crest Investment Trust, Inc. v. Comstock, 23 Md. App. 280, 327 A.2d 891 (1974).

3. Commonwealth v. Davis, 364 Mass. 555, 307 N.E.2d 6 (1974).

4. Smith v. Lewis, 13 Cal.3d 349, 530 P.2d 589, 118 Cal. Rptr. 621 (1975).

5. Spector v. Mermelstein, 485 F.2d 474 (2d. Cir. 1973).

6. Sitton v. Clements, 385 F.2d 869 (6th Cir. 1967).

7. Denzer v. Rouse, 48 Wis.2d 528, 180 N.W.2d 521 (1970); Grago v. Robertson, 49 App. Div. 2d 645, 370 N.Y.S.2d 255 (3d Dept. 1975); Martin v. Burns, 102 Ariz. 341, 429 P.2d 660 (1967); Baker v. Beal, —— Iowa ——, 225 N.W.2d 106 (1975).

8. Cook, Flanagan and Berst v. Clausing, 73 Wash.2d 393, 438 P.2d 865 (1968); *in re* Cronin, 133 Vt. 234, 336 A.2d 164 (1975).

9. Spector, *supra* note 5; Creative Inception, Inc. v. Andrews, 50 App.Div.2d 553, 377 N.Y.S.2d 1 (1st Dept. 1975) (damages must be proved with reasonable certainty); Christy v. Saliterman, 288 Minn. 144, 179 N.W.2d 288 (1970) (in malpractice action for failure to bring timely suit, the client was required to prove that if the suit had been brought, he would have prevailed).

10. Fisk v. Newsum, 9 Wash. App. 650, 513 P.2d 1035 (1973); Shelly v. Hansen, 244 Cal. App. 2d 210, 53 Cal. Rptr. 20 (1966).

11. Blackmon v. Hale, 1 Cal.3d 548, 463 P.2d 418, 83 Cal. Rptr. 194 (1970).

12. N.Y. BUS. CORP. LAW § 1505(a) (McKinney).

13. McDow v. Dixon, 138 Ga. App. 338, 226 S.E.2d 145 (1976); Hansen v. Wightman, 14 Wash. App. 78, 538 P.2d 1238 (1975).

14. Martin v. Hall, 20 Cal. App. 3d 414, 97 Cal. Rptr. 730, 53 A.L.R.3d 719 (1971).

15. McEvoy v. Helikson, 277 Or. 781, 562 P.2d 540 (1977).

16. Goodman v. Kennedy, 18 Cal.3d 335, 556 P.2d 737, 134 Cal. Rptr. 375 (1976).

17. Lucas v. Hamm, 56 Cal.2d 583, 364 P.2d 685, 15 Cal. Rptr. 821 (1961), *cert. denied*, 368 U.S. 987 (1962); Heyer v. Flaig, 70 Cal.2d 223, 449 P.2d 161, 74 Cal. Rptr. 225 (1969).

18. Victor v. Goldman, 74 Misc. 2d 685, 344 N.Y.S.2d 672 (Sup. Ct. Rockland County 1973), *aff'd*, 43 App. Div. 2d 1021, 351 N.Y.S.2d 956 (2d Dept. 1974).

19. Adams v. American W. Sec., Inc., 265 Or. 514, 510 P.2d 838, 62 A.L.R.3d 240 (1973). *Cf.* S.E.C. v. National

Student Mktg. Corp., 402 F. Supp. 641 (D.D.C. 1975) ——
F. Supp. —— (D.D.C. Aug. 31, 1978).

20. Donald v. Garry, 19 Cal. App. 3d 769, 97 Cal. Rptr. 191, 45 A.L.R.3d 1177 (1971).

21. Capital Bank & Trust Co. v. Core, 343 So. 2d 284 (La. App. 1977); Collins v. Fitzwater, 277 Or. 401, 560 P.2d 1074 (1977).

22. Hahn v. Wylie, 54 App.Div.2d 629, 387 N.Y.S.2d 855, 856 (1st Dept. 1976).

23. N.Y. CIV. PRAC. LAW § 214 (McKinney).

24. CAL. CIV. PROC. CODE § 339 (1) (Deering).

25. *See, e.g.*, Peters v. Simmons, 87 Wash.2d 400, 552 P.2d 1053 (1976). *Cf.* Heyer, *supra* note 17.

26. *In* re Phillips, 510 F.2d 126 (2nd Cir. 1975).

27. Ames v. State Bar of Cal., 8 Cal.3d 910, 506 P.2d 625, 106 Cal. Rptr. 489 (1973). *See also* Melson v. Michlin, 43 Del. Ch. 239, 223 A.2d 338 (1966); Toledo Bar Ass'n v. Miller, 22 Ohio St. 2d 7, 257 N.E.2d 376 (1970). *Cf.* Nadler v. Treptow, —— Iowa ——, 166 N.W.2d 103 (1969), *in re* Bond & Mtge. Guar. Co., 303 N.Y. 423, 103 N.E.2d 721 (1952); Sea Cove Marina, Inc. v. Uhlendorf, 18 App. Div. 2d 1021, 239 N.Y.S.2d 29 (2d Dept. 1963), *aff'd*, 15 N.Y.2d 714, 204 N.E.2d 499, 256 N.Y.2d 340 1965); Hafter v. Farkas, 498 F.2d 587 (2d Cir. 1974).

28. Yokozeki v. State Bar of Cal., 11 Cal. 3d 436, 521 P.2d 858, 113 Cal. Rptr. 602 (1974), *cert. denied,* 419 U.S. 900 (1974); S.E.C. v. W.L. Moody & Co., 363 F. Supp. 481 (S.D. Tex. 1973); Udall v. Littell, 366 F.2d 668 (D.C. Cir. 1966), *cert. denied,* 385 U.S. 1007 (1967).

29. Parker v. Williams Construction Co., 443 F.2d 597 (9th Cir. 1971); *in re* Anderson, 52 Ill. 2d 202, 287 N.E.2d 682 (1972); Rogers v. Niforatos, 57 App. Div. 2d 984, 394 N.Y.S.2d 473 (3rd Dept. 1977) (former client).

30. Melson, *supra* note 27; Iula v. Grampa, 257 Md. 370, 263 A.2d 548 (1970); Pasternak v. Mashak, —— Mo. ——, 428 S.W.2d 565 (1967), *cert. denied,* 390 U.S. 907 (1968).

31. Greenberg v. Bar Steel Constr. Corp., 22 N.Y.2d 210, 239 N.E.2d 343, 292 N.Y.S.2d 404 (1968).

32. Kennedy v. Clausing, 74 Wash.2d 483, 445 P.2d 637 (1968).

33. Gold v. Greenwald, 247 Cal. App. 2d 296, 55 Cal. Rptr. 660 (1966).

34. Cuthbert v. Heidsieck, —— Mo. ——, 364 S.W.2d 583 (1963) (court voids gift of $19,975 worth of stock given by eighty-year-old client to attorney); Magee v. State Bar of Cal., 58 Cal.2d 423, 374 P.2d 807, 24 Cal. Rptr. 839 (1962) (causing client to give attorney gift or to mention

him in client's will through the use of undue influence is a disciplinable violation).

35. Hafter, *supra* note 27; *in re* Smiley, 286 Ala. 216, 238 So. 2d 716 (1970); *in re* Bretz, 168 Mont. 23, 542 P.2d 1227 (1975); Kaplan v. Bobick, 26 App. Div. 2d 783, 273 N.Y.S.2d 648 (1st Dept. 1966).
36. *In re* Gerrick, 36 App. Div. 2d 508, 321 N.Y.S.2d 662 (1st Dept. 1971); *in re* Hannon, 214 Or. 51, 324 P.2d 753 (1958).
37. *See, generally,* Annot., Wills: Undue Influence in Gift to Testator's Attorney, 19 A.L.R.3d 575-634 (1968).

IX

Limits on Advocacy, Including First-Amendment Rights of Lawyers and Clients

Do clients have a constitutional right to organize in order to make it easier to use the courts?

Yes. The precise scope of this right is not yet defined by the cases. But it is clear that a broad right exists and that citizens may take certain action in order to exercise that right. The leading cases in the area deal with the right of citizens to organize to have their common interest protected by the courts. In *NAACP* v. *Button,* the United States Supreme Court ruled that a state's valid interest in regulating the profession of law could not justify interference with the constitutionally protected activities of the NAACP in financing litigation aimed at ending racial segregation in the public schools. The state of Virginia saw the NAACP's activities as "soliciting" legal business. The court held, however, that the activity of the NAACP in counseling minority group members in Virginia about violation of their rights and referring them to a particular attorney or group of attorneys for assistance is protected by the First Amendment to the United States Constitution.[1]

In two subsequent cases, the Supreme Court made it clear that the First Amendment protection was not limited

147

to organizing to bring civil rights cases. Unions could hire lawyers to represent their members in workmen's compensation and similar cases. Unions could also have arrangements with attorneys under which the attorney, in exchange for referrals by the union, would promise not to charge union members more than a certain maximum percentage of any recovery in a workmen's compensation or related case. The union's valid interest in providing its members with competent counsel at reasonable fees was constitutionally protected. But, as the court held in one of these cases,

> the principle here involved cannot be limited to the facts of this case. At issue is the basic right to group legal action, a right first asserted in this Court by an association of Negroes seeking the protection of freedoms guaranteed by the Constitution. The common thread running through our decisions ... is that collective activity undertaken to obtain meaningful access to the courts is a fundamental right within the protection of the First Amendment. However, that right would be a hollow promise if courts could deny associations of workers or others the means of enabling their members to meet the costs of legal representation.[2]

Since these decisions, there has been much talk of experimentation with various plans under which groups of otherwise unrelated or only marginally related citizens join forces in order to purchase lawyer time for less money. These plans have been called "judicare," legal insurance, group practice, and so on. This development is still in its infancy. Much remains to be done and much of whatever will be done will have to be accomplished through public pressure. The American Bar Association has shown itself highly reluctant to alter its Code of Professional Responsibility to make group legal practice or legal insurance more feasible. Still, some bar associations and some unions are experimenting in this area and some courts have approved their efforts.[3]

LIMITS ON ADVOCACY

Do nonlawyers have a first amendment right to tell other nonlawyers what their legal rights are?

Generally not. This is discussed in the questions dealing with the unauthorized practice of law in the next chapter. But there is some change going on here. One Court recently said that a tenant's union had a first amendment right to give accurate, ethical advice to tenant members on their rights. This is a bold decision, which one hopes will be followed.[4]

How far can a lawyer go in representing her client?

A lawyer has an affirmative obligation, stated in the Code of Professional Responsibility, to represent her client "zealously." However, the same canon of the Code also contains a qualifier—the lawyer's representation must be "within the bounds of the law." Among the limitations imposed by the qualifier are the following. The lawyer is not permitted to take a position merely to harass or maliciously injure another. She is not permitted knowingly to advance an unwarranted legal claim. She may not knowingly use perjured testimony or false evidence or knowingly make a false statement of law or fact.[5]

Every once in a while, cases arise dealing with conduct by lawyers that go beyond what is required by the obligation to represent a client "zealously." In one recent case, for example, a lawyer representing an alien filed a petition for review of a decision ordering the alien deported. The court found the petition "to be so utterly frivolous and completely lacking in any merit as to permit but one conclusion: that it was interposed solely as a delaying tactic by counsel who was well aware of its meritlessness." The court wrote that the obligation to represent a client zealously "does not justify the assertion of frivolous positions in litigation." The court assessed double costs of the appeal to be paid by the attorney personally.[6]

If the client is perpetrating a fraud upon a tribunal or another person, his lawyer may find himself in a quandary. The ethical rules at one time required that the lawyer call upon the client to rectify the fraud and, if the client refused, to reveal the fraud to the person or tribunal.[7] The American Bar Association subsequently amended this ethical provision so that the lawyer need not reveal the fraud "when the information is protected as a privileged communication."[8] Not all state bar associations have adopted this exception. In a recent case, the Supreme Court of Oregon ruled that where a lawyer concludes that his client is perpetrating a fraud on a court or another person, the lawyer is obligated to withdraw from the representation if the client will not rectify the fraud, though the lawyer need not reveal the fraud if to do so would violate confidential information.[9] Some commentators have argued that a criminal-defense lawyer does not have an ethical obligation to correct perjury by his client and does not have an ethical obligation to withdraw from the case if the client refuses to correct it.[10] No grievance committee or court has yet accepted this position.

Can a lawyer bring litigation to delay his client's obligation to pay money?

No. It is a violation of professional ethics to use the courts "solely as a dilatory tactic to avoid paying a judgment." The courts can and often have awarded damages and other monetary relief to persons against whom the courts were so used.[11]

Can a lawyer use electronic surveillance?

No, according to the bar associations that have issued formal opinions on this subject. (The only one to permit it is the Texas Bar Association.) The American Bar Association has said that "no lawyer should record any conversation whether by tapes or other electronic device, without the consent or prior knowledge of all parties to the conversation."[12] The ABA opinion acknowledges that it is not necessarily a violation of the law to make such recordings.

Can a lawyer ever tell his client to disobey a court order?

Practically never. Court orders must be obeyed. If a lawyer believes the order is incorrect, he can appeal and seek a stay. But he cannot advise his client to disregard it. Of course, a lawyer can object to a ruling, but once the court has ruled, the directive must be followed. One exception to this involves the Fifth Amendment privilege against self-incrimination. In a recent case, the court ordered a witness to reveal certain information which the lawyer believed to be privileged under the Fifth Amendment. The attorney advised his client not to reveal the information, but rather to disobey the court order and appeal it, risking a contempt citation if he lost the appeal. The client took his lawyer's advice, and the trial judge held the lawyer in contempt.

"The privilege against compelled self-incrimination," said the Supreme Court in reversing the contempt, "would be drained of its meaning if counsel, being lawfully present, as here, could be penalized for advising his client in good faith to assert it." The court continued:

> The witness, once advised of the right, can choose for himself whether to risk contempt in order to test the privilege before evidence is produced. That decision is, and should be, for the witness. But, if his lawyer may be punished for advice so given there is a genuine risk that a witness exposed to possible self-incrimination will not be advised of his right.[13]

Can a lawyer testify for her own client?

The ethical rules prohibit a lawyer from accepting a case if she or someone in her firm "ought to be called as a witness" should there be a trial. There are exceptions if the testimony will relate solely to uncontested matters, matters of formality solely, the nature and value of legal services rendered in the case, or if refusal of employment would cause a "substantial hardship on the client."[14] Likewise, if in the course of a representation, a lawyer learns that he or someone in his firm "ought to be called as a witness" he has a similar obligation to withdraw.[15] Numerous cases strictly enforce this rule.[16]

Will an attorney be disciplined simply for filing a complaint that turns out to be frivolous?

The Code of Professional Responsibility makes it a disciplinary violation to "knowingly advance a claim or defense that is unwarranted under existing law," unless the claim or defense "can be supported by good faith argument for an extension, modification, or reversal of existing law."[17] It is obviously unacceptable for lawyers to have to take a risk, whenever they assert a novel theory, that they will be subject to discipline if the court does not buy their argument. If this were so, lawyers would be most cautious about breaking new ground, and the law would not grow. On the other hand, the courts are willing to impose sanctions when a lawyer files a frivolous claim or defense, in order to gain a collateral advantage, knowing of the frivolity of the claim or defense. In one case, the United States Court of Appeals for the First Circuit suspended a lawyer who filed frivolous petitions for review in immigration cases, some of which he did not even bother to pursue. The mere filing of the petition operated to stay deportation. The lawyer had been previously warned about such conduct.[18]

Can a lawyer attack the motives or bias of a judge?

Yes, within limits. In one case, a judge ordered a lawyer to show cause why he should not be held in contempt. The lawyer asked the judge to disqualify himself from trying the contempt case. The judge declined. The lawyer then moved to change the place of trial and hired a second lawyer to represent him. In making the motion to change the place of trial, the lawyers filed a document attacking the trial judge. Among other things, it accused him of acting "as police officer, chief prosecution witness, adverse witness for the defense, grand jury, chief prosecutor, and judge." It also accused him of intimidating and harassing the lawyer charged with contempt, seriously hampering his efforts to defend himself. Both lawyers were subsequently fined for contempt because of the language of the motion seeking a change of place of trial. The United States Supreme Court reversed. The court wrote that

> the words used in the motions were plain English, in no way offensive in themselves, and wholly appropriate to charge bias in the community and bias of the presiding judge. . . . But if the charges were "insulting" it was inherent in the issue of bias raised, an issue which we have seen had to be raised, according to the charges, to escape the probability of a constitutionally unfair trial.[19]

In another case, where a lawyer urged a judge to disqualify himself for bias, a new judge declined to find the lawyer in contempt although it was a "difficult" question. The lawyer had charged the judge with having already made up his mind. Among other things, the lawyer said that "I fully believe, and with all due respect to the Court as a person, that you made up your mind about everything except the length of the sentence." While the court did not find the lawyer in contempt, it did say that "there would seem to be no need for a lawyer to use words of the kind respondent used."[20]

The court will likely find contempt if there is (1) misbehavior, (2) occurring before or near the judge, (3) sufficiently obstructionist to interfere with the administration of justice, and (4) done intentionally. The obstruction of justice must be "actual, not theoretical."[21]

Can an attorney's comments be so outrageous that the elements of obstruction and intent are established merely by virtue of what the attorney has said?

Yes. In some cases, there can be conduct that is "so outrageous that it unmistakably established by its own presence both intent and obstruction."[22] Furthermore, "the manner in which insulting remarks, not obstructive of themselves, are levelled may accomplish an obstruction. For example, shouting the remarks or accompanying their utterance with physical demonstration may provide the necessary element." Finally, there can be a "material obstruction" simply as a result of the "delay of the proceedings occasioned by a disrespectful outburst or other misbehavior."[23]

Statements by the United States Supreme Court in a contempt case involving a defendant, not an attorney, are also appropriate. It is true that defendants enjoy the arguably greater protection of the First Amendment, while lawyers are bound by ethical requirements. But in one recent case, the Supreme Court ruled that in order for a defendant (who was representing himself without counsel) to be found guilty of contempt, his comments "must constitute an imminent, not merely a likely, threat to the administration of justice. The danger must not be remote or even probable; it must immediately imperil. . . . The law of contempt is not made for the protection of judges who may be sensitive to the winds of public opinion." And the court continued: "Trial courts . . . must be on guard against confusing offenses to their sensibilities with obstruction to the administration of justice."[24]

What are some examples of comments by attorneys that have resulted in contempt citations?

Many of the successful contempt prosecutions against attorneys for comments to the trial judge occur in state courts. For example, in one California Supreme Court case, a contempt citation was upheld where, after the trial judge denied an attorney's motion, the lawyer responded: "This court obviously doesn't want to apply the law." The California Supreme Court said that it was

> settled law of this state that an attorney commits a direct contempt when he impugns the integrity of the court by statements made in open court either orally or in writing. . . . Insolence to the judge in the form of insulting words or conduct in court has traditionally been recognized in the common law as constituting grounds for contempt. . . . Applying the foregoing authorities to the matter before us, we think it is manifest that petitioner's statement constituted an attack on the integrity of the court.[25]

Charges of judicial incompetency, dishonesty, and partiality, and personal attacks on a judge have all been ruled sufficient to sustain contempt motions.[26] In short, to the extent that a lawyer questions a judge's partiality, skills, or fairness as necessarily incidental to a valid motion or to preserve a legal position, it seems that the comments will not be held grounds for contempt. Some courts even allow an attorney to go beyond this. But gratuitous attacks on particular judges, without any collateral legal purpose, will sustain summary criminal-contempt findings.

To what extent can an attorney criticize a particular judge, the courts, or the judicial system outside the courtroom?

Here, lawyers have broader freedom, at least in some

states. In one Kansas case, an attorney who had earlier been disciplined made a public statement to a newspaper reporter that he felt "complimented" by the allegations against him and that he had "very little respect for the police and the courts." He charged that the courts "are commonly prejudiced and they're much more concerned with who appears before them than what the facts are, and the law is." The court, in declining to discipline the lawyer for this remark, said that

> while a lawyer may, in a proper tone and through appropriate channels, attack the integrity or competence of a court or a judge, or the propriety of any particular judicial act, he may not, by unfounded charges, create disrespect for courts or their decisions and if he does so he may be properly disciplined.

Criticism was acceptable but "misrepresentation and unwarranted assaults on the courts" are not. The court considered it important that the lawyer was responding to a reporter's question. The lawyer did not seek out the reporter. The remarks were against law enforcement and judicial institutions generally and not against any particular person. The court was also impressed with the fact that the lawyer himself, rather than a client, was the actual litigant.[27]

While the lawyer in this case may have just squeaked through, a subsequent New York case provides much greater latitude. A lawyer who had been defending criminals for the Legal Aid Society for twenty-five years was interviewed by *Life* magazine. Among other things, he said: "There are so few trial judges who just judge, who rule on questions of law, and leave guilt or innocence to the jury." He then went on to call appellate judges "the whores who became madams." He said that he would like to be a judge "to see if I could be the kind of judge I think a judge should be. But the only way you can get it is to be in politics or buy it—and I don't even know the going price." Finally, the lawyer said: "I have nothing to do with justice. Justice is not even part of the equation. If you say I have no moral reaction to what I do, you are right." In a five-to-two decision, the New York Court of Appeals reversed a lower court decision finding the lawyer guilty of ethical violations deserving of censure. The court said that standing alone,

> isolated instances of disrespect for the law, judges, and courts expressed by vulgar and insulting words or other incivility, uttered, written, or committed outside the precincts of a court are not subject to professional discipline. . . . Nor is the matter substantially altered if there is hyperbole expressed in the impoverished vocabulary of the street.

But the court did indicate that there were limits. "Perhaps persistent or general courses of conduct, even if parading as criticism, which are degrading to the law, the bar, and the courts, and are irrelevant or grossly excessive, would present a different issue."[28]

Other lawyers have been less successful. In a Nevada case, the prosecutor was reprimanded after he characterized an opinion of the state supreme court as shocking and stated, among other things, that the opinion was an example of judicial legislation.[29]

Do attorneys enjoy the same First Amendment protections for their out-of-court statements that ordinary citizens do?

It is not clear. Courts have gone both ways. The most recent United States Supreme Court decision in a case involving this issue seemed to indicate that the attorney's professional obligations may circumscribe his or her First Amendment rights.[30] But this decision is nearly twenty years old. Since then, some courts have rejected that notion.[31] On the other hand, other courts continue to maintain that an attorney can be disciplined for out-of-court statements which are protected by the First Amendment but held to violate the attorney's oath of office.[32]

Is it possible to predict what the courts will do in this area?

Not with any certainty. The cases seem to indicate that the courts will take the following factors into consideration where an attorney makes a critical out-of-court statement.

LIMITS ON ADVOCACY

1. Is the statement made with regard to a pending matter or a matter that has already concluded? If the matter is concluded, the likelihood of discipline is less.
2. Is the statement, though critical, based on reason or analysis? If it is, the likelihood of discipline is less, even if it is wrong or even if others will disagree with it. On the other hand, if the statement is emotional or hysterical or attacks the courts or particular judges in an irrational way, the likelihood of discipline is greater.
3. Is the statement directed toward a named person or persons? If it is, the likelihood of discipline will be greater, since the harm is greater and since, in the case of a judge at least, the ability to respond is limited.
4. What are the circumstances giving rise to the statement? If the attorney instigates the publication of the remarks, the chances of discipline are greater than if the attorney is simply approached by others for his opinion.
5. To the extent that critical comments are made repeatedly without basis, the chances of discipline are greater than if the criticism is a single occurrence.

Can a lawyer make an out-of-court statement about a trial in progress if the statement does not attack anybody?

This question raises the issue of the validity of "gag" orders, under which trial judges have prohibited lawyers (and litigants) from speaking to the press about an ongoing trial. Trial courts have used this tool to protect against pretrial publicity and publicity during the trial, because there are stringent limitations on the ability of the courts directly to prohibit the press from printing information about a pending case.[33] The traditional rule has been that gag orders or "no-comment" ethical rules (that is, rules requiring lawyers to answer "no comment" when questioned by the press about pending matters) are constitutional and within the power of the court to impose. Indeed, that is still the rule in most jurisdictions.[34]

Some courts, however, have moved away from the traditional test and have prohibited the use of no-comment rules, and by implication, gag orders, in those circumstances where direct restraint on the press itself would not be constitutionally permitted. The leading case in this area comes from the United States Court of Appeals for the Seventh Circuit. This case involved the validity of the no-comment rules of the federal court of Chicago. The Seventh Circuit ruled that it was not permissible to proscribe lawyers' comments about pending or imminent litigation simply because "there is a reasonable likelihood that such dissemination will interfere with a fair trial or otherwise prejudice the due administration of justice." The court felt this was "overbroad and therefore does not meet constitutional standards." Instead, the court ruled that "only those comments that pose a 'serious and imminent threat' of interference with the fair administration of justice can be constitutionally proscribed."[35] Other courts have rejected this position and have maintained that a gag order or no-comment rule can be applied to attorneys if the proscribed comments are "reasonably likely" to interfere with a fair trial or prejudice the due administration of justice.[36]

This problem has an interesting twist. The extensive list of prohibitions on what a lawyer may say while a case is in progress is contained in Disciplinary Rule 7-107 of the Code of Professional Responsibility. This rule does not provide any standard against which the attorney can judge his statements. In other words, the rule says that the attorney shall make no comment regarding a host of matters whether or not the comment has any effect on the administration of justice at all. So while the courts are splitting between a position (a) requiring the attorney's comments to create a "serious and imminent threat" to the administration of justice before they can be restricted, and a position which (b) permits restriction if the comments are simply "reasonably likely" to interfere with the administration of justice, the disciplinary rule itself contains neither of these qualifications.

A New York court recently recognized that the absence of any qualification at all would make the rule unconstitutional. That court took the stricter position and ruled that an attorney's out-of-court statements could not be restricted unless they presented a "clear and present danger to the administration of justice." Indeed, said the court, "only where the words used present a clear and present danger, can it be said that there is a likelihood of interference with a fair trial."[37]

What kind of statements is a lawyer prohibited from making to the press during the course of a trial?

Whichever test is used—the "reasonable likelihood" test, the "serious and imminent threat" test, or the "clear and present danger" test—the substance of what a lawyer is not permitted to talk about is spelled out in Disciplinary Rule 7-107, which has been adopted by all bar associations in one form or another. This rule prohibits a lawyer, defense or prosecution, involved in a criminal case from discussing the character, reputation, or prior criminal record of the accused, the possibility of a plea of guilty, the existence or contents of any confession, the results of any scientific tests, the identity, testimony or credibility of prospective witnesses, his opinion of the guilt or innocence of the accused, or the merits of the case. Exceptions include information contained in the public record, the fact that an investigation is in progress, the scope of the investigation, a request for public assistance, a warning of danger, the name, age, and other data about the accused, information that would assist in apprehending the accused, circumstances surrounding the arrest, the identity of the arresting officers, a description of evidence seized, the nature and substance of the charge, and that the accused denies the charges made against him. Similar rules apply to civil trials and administrative proceedings.

In the *Chicago Council of Lawyers* case, the court specifically held that it was not permissible to prohibit a lawyer from stating his belief that a statute is unjust.

It must be emphasized, however, that even a comment falling within the definitions of Disciplinary Rule 7-107 is protected by the free-speech provisions of the First Amendment, even in the most conservative and traditional jurisdictions, unless there is a "reasonable likelihood" that the comment will prejudice the administration of justice. In some jurisdictions, as we have pointed out, the comment is protected even if there is such a likelihood, so long as there is not a "serious and imminent threat" or "clear

THE RIGHTS OF LAWYERS AND CLIENTS

and present danger" that it will interfere with the fair administration of justice.

After a lawyer begins a lawsuit, can she notify the press about it?

Yes, if she is careful. It doesn't matter if the newspaper report mentions the lawyer by name. But if a lawyer deliberately encourages publicity in order to promote her name or private interests, she can be disciplined.[38] A lawyer can also use the press to attempt to find witnesses or persons situated similarly to her client who might be interested in pursuing a class action. It may be, however, in these circumstances, that the client rather than the lawyer should be the moving force.[39] Note, however, that this entire area may be in for substantial change as a result of new rules regulating lawyers' advertising, as discussed next.

Can lawyers advertise?

For a long time the answer to this question was *no*. Now the answer to this question is *sometimes*. The United States Supreme Court has recently held that, at least under certain circumstances, it is a violation of the First Amendment for a state to impose disciplinary sanctions on a lawyer who advertises. The advertisement involved in the Supreme Court case was in a newspaper. It listed routine legal services such as uncontested divorces, adoptions, bankruptcy, and name change. It also provided price information for each of these services. The advertisement gave the name of the law firm ("Legal Clinic of Bates & O'Steen"), its address, and its telephone number. The advertisement offered information "regarding other types of cases, on request." The advertisement also said that the firm would provide "legal services at very reasonable fees." As a result of this advertisement, the two lawyers in the firm were censured.

The United States Supreme Court reversed the censure. The court rejected the following arguments in support of the ban on lawyer advertisement:

1. advertising adversely affected professionalism;
2. legal advertising is inherently misleading;

3. legal advertising will have an adverse effect on the administration of justice;
4. legal advertising will have undesirable effects on the cost of legal services;
5. legal advertising will have adverse effects on the quality of legal services;
6. it is difficult to enforce rules regarding legal advertising.

The court concluded that advertising by attorneys "may not be subjected to blanket suppression." But there can be limitations. "Advertising that is false, deceptive, or misleading" is subject to restraint. The court also noted that advertising claims "as to the quality of services" were not as "susceptible to measurement or verification" and might therefore "be so likely to be misleading as to warrant restriction." But the court did not rule on this issue. Nor did it rule on the validity of "in-person solicitation," or whether the state may validly require lawyers to place some "warning or disclaimer or the like" on legal advertising. The court also did not deal with whether "advertising on the electronic broadcast media will warrant special consideration." Indeed, the court specifically limited its holding (from which four of the nine justices dissented) to a conclusion that the state could not "prevent the publication in a newspaper of [the lawyers'] truthful advertisement concerning the availability and terms of routine legal services."

The decision therefore can be read narrowly, especially since it was rendered by a bare majority of the court. It involves advertisement of routine services, in print media, containing only truthful, objective information, and making no representations about quality.[40]

How about lawyers who write best-selling books and get their names in advertisements for the books?

This has never been condemned. In fact, there are apparently no reported cases dealing with such conduct. In one case dealing with a related area, attorney Melvin Belli hired a lecture bureau to get lecture appearances for him, for which he would be paid a fee. The lecture bureau prepared brochures and distributed thousands of them around the country to persons and institutions likely to be interested in hiring lecturers. The court held that this alone did not violate the rules of professional conduct since there was no showing that Belli said or did anything at the lectures constituting solicitation of legal business. The brochures and the lectures were not a subterfuge to build Belli's law practice. On the other hand, it was a disciplinary violation for the attorney to permit the lecture bureau to send out letters to the news media praising the lawyer's talents and stating that personalities and former clients would pay tribute to the lawyer at a celebration. The court concluded that the letters constituted a disciplinary violation because they suggested Belli had performed his services "so well that his clients consequently praise him." This was not allowed. Finally, it was also a disciplinary violation for Belli to have allowed himself to appear in advertisements for a brand of Scotch whiskey. Belli was suspended for thirty days.[41] The decision in this case was limited by the California court in the case discussed in the answer to the next question.

What will be the effect of decisions like *Bates* on cases like *Belli*?

Probably the decision in *Belli v. State Bar of California* is still valid only for a very narrow principle. Even before the United States Supreme Court decided the *Bates* case, the California Supreme Court had to deal with a disciplinary proceeding against a law firm that purported to operate as a "legal clinic." Under this title, the law firm sought to provide routine services to a high-volume clientele. The two lawyers in the firm cooperated with news media in the publication of articles and the broadcasting of stories about their clinic. They were brought up on disciplinary charges. A month before the Supreme Court's *Bates* decision, the California Supreme Court held that the activity of the lawyers was protected by the First Amendment. The California Supreme Court relied on earlier United States Supreme Court decisions, holding that commercial speech was protected under the First Amendment.

The California court's decision is even broader than the *Bates* decision. First, the California court strictly limited the *Belli* decision to only those situations where a lawyer's activity serves no discernible purpose other than to attract clients. If there is any other legitimate purpose to the activity, it is protected by the First Amendment, even if the activity also attracts clients and even if the lawyer is aware of this. Second, the legitimate state interest in protecting against misleading or false advertising applies only to paid advertisements by lawyers directly soliciting clients. The same danger is not present where the lawyer cooperates with a journalist in the publication or broadcast of a news story.

On balance, the court concluded that the news articles about the legal clinic served a legitimate purpose because they brought an important issue to the attention of the public. The court would therefore not analyze what other motives the lawyers may have had. To hold otherwise, the court stressed, would require scrutiny of the motives of lawyers who write books about their major cases, lawyers who become political candidates even when they can't win, and lawyers who participate in community activities calculated to bring their names to public attention.[42]

Have bar associations proposed rules governing advertising in light of the Supreme Court's Bates decision?

Yes. The focus in the battle over whether advertising will be permitted has now shifted to how it should be controlled. There are two clear camps and many positions in between. One side believes that there should be no restriction on advertising so long as the advertisements are not misleading, fraudulent, or the like. The other side wants advertising to be as "professional" and dignified as possible. The two points of view are expressed in the different proposals of the American Bar Association following the Supreme Court decision. One proposal is basically "regulatory." As the ABA describes it, "it would specifically authorize certain prescribed forms of lawyer advertising if approved by state authorities." The other proposal is "directive." The ABA describes this proposal as allowing "publication of all information not 'false, fraudulent, misleading, or deceptive' and provides guidelines for determination of improper advertisements." The alternate proposals have been published.[43] The New York State Bar Association has opted for a "regulatory" approach in proposing rules to the state courts for adoption.[44] The state bar rules would permit print and radio advertisement, but, pending further study, no television. The kind of information the state rules would permit include name, address, telephone, biographical and educational information, public offices held, military service, publications, teaching positions, professional memberships, foreign-language ability, bank references, names of clients regularly represented if they consent, office hours, credit arrangements, certain fee information, and claimed areas of specialization.

What about solicitation?

Solicitation will be the next area debated after advertising. It is not always clear what the difference is. In theory, advertising seeks to reach a large number of unidentified people, while solicitation involves an approach to a comparatively smaller number of identifiable people. For example, an announcement in a magazine, even a specialty magazine, aims at all readers. But a form letter written to a dozen (or even a hundred) people injured in a particular accident aims only at specific individuals. The first is advertising, the second is solicitation. The distinction, however, is not always so clear. Nevertheless, the courts will have to tackle the problem of solicitation and soon. The Illinois Supreme Court has already ruled that an attorney is not guilty of professional misconduct because he mailed communications to about two thousand present and former clients asking them to notify him of any change of address, describing his practice, and offering advice on a range of subjects.[45]

Solicitation also occurs in the area of class actions, since the attorney for the class representative may wish to find others to participate in the litigation. He may therefore attempt to contact them in any number of ways to solicit financial or other support for the action. This has been held protected.[46]

Solicitation also involves the famous lawyer bugaboo: the ambulance-chaser. The Supreme Court recently upheld discipline in a "classic" solicitation case. In this case an Ohio lawyer learned that two young women whom he knew casually had been involved in an auto accident. He visited both and offered to represent them in a personal-injury lawsuit. He taped his conversation with at least one of the women without her knowledge. He was eventually charged with solicitation and suspended from practice indefinitely. The Supreme Court affirmed.[47]

At the same time, the Supreme Court considered a "solicitation" case from the opposite end of the spectrum. A young woman lawyer, acting as a volunteer for the American Civil Liberties Union, wrote to a welfare mother in South Carolina offering to have the ACLU bring a lawsuit on the woman's behalf, without fee, for damages arising out of the apparent fact that the prospective client had been sterilized without her consent. The lawyer was censured by the South Carolina Supreme Court. The Supreme Court reversed.[48]

The United States Supreme Court's resolution of the Ohio and South Carolina cases should further define the limits on attorney solicitation. Nevertheless, this is truly a murky area where any prediction is risky.[49]

Are there limits on what a lawyer can wear to court?

There are certainly limits, although the issue is not often litigated. In one interesting recent case, a Roman Catholic priest, who was also a criminal defense lawyer working for the Legal Aid Society, wore clerical garb to court to try a criminal case before a jury. The New York Court of Appeals ruled that the trial judge could properly forbid this. The lawyer's function, the court said, is "not to displace his client but to serve as his agent in the litigation." By wearing clerical garb, the lawyer tends to "substitute himself for the client before the jury or court." The trial judge has power to regulate the attire of the lawyer "when that regulation is reasonably related to the preservation of order and decorum in the courtroom, the protection of the rights of parties and witnesses, and generally to the furtherance of the administration of justice." The court noted that the case did not present the more difficult question of "nonclerical religious practices, symbols, and expressions which might be presented, or which might invoke absolutes of religious doctrine, in the tableau of a judicial trial."[50]

Can a judge require that a lawyer dress with a certain degree of formality or in a certain style when appearing in court?

Yes. But there are limitations. In a Florida case, a lawyer was found in contempt of court and sent to jail for three days because he appeared in the courtroom without a necktie. The judge had ordered him to wear a tie in court. The lawyer responded: "No sir. I am saying right now I shall not. I shall dress my mode of dress, not the dictations of the Court." When the lawyer next appeared in court before the same judge, he wore a white suit, a sport shirt open at the neck, and a necklace with a round gold pendant the size of a silver dollar "with the hair on his chest showing through the open shirt." The judge adjourned court for an hour so the lawyer could change. But when the lawyer returned, he was dressed in the same way. He was then found in contempt. The appellate court ruled that a judge had the power to impose dress requirements upon lawyers appearing before him in judicial proceedings. Requiring the lawyer to wear a tie would not violate due-process or equal-protection guarantees of the federal Constitution. As long as the court's action was reasonably related to a "justifiable end or purpose," it could be upheld.[51]

In another case, a woman lawyer wore a miniskirt to court, with the hemline five inches above her knee. The judge ordered her to leave the court until her dress was "suitable, conventional, and appropriate." The appellate court acknowledged that a judge does have authority to control behavior in his courtroom, including dress. But here there was no showing that the lawyer's miniskirt in any way created distraction or in any manner disrupted the orderly proceedings of the court. There was no suggestion that "[her] dress was so immodest or revealing as to shock one's sense of propriety." Before a judge can order a lawyer to dress in a certain way, the record must show "factual conditions which leave no doubt that a continuance of the proscribed conduct will result in a disrespect for order and an impairment in the administration of justice."[52]

In a similar case, a New Jersey appellate court reversed the contempt conviction of a female lawyer who had worn gray wool slacks, a matching gray sweater, and a green open-collared blouse to court. This dress could not "be fairly labeled disruptive, distractive, or depreciative of the solemnity of the judicial process."[53]

Can a judge control the appearance of litigants?

Theoretically, yes, if the dress of a litigant interferes with the orderly administration of justice. In one recent case, two defendants in traffic court, though neatly attired, were not dressed in accordance with court rules requiring men to wear jackets, ties, and slacks. They were held in contempt. The appellate court reversed since it could not be said that the dress was "unsuitable, unconventional, or inappropriate" or that it "tended to interfere with the orderly administration of justice." In another case a court held that a Jewish civil litigant had a right to wear his skull cap in court.[54]

Can lawyers who work for a legal-aid society or other public or quasi-public institutions strike?

Yes, under certain circumstances, according to the New York County Lawyers' Association's Committee on Professional Ethics. But the lawyers may not strike "if doing so either disrupts the proper functioning of the courts and the judicial system or deprives indigent defendants of their right to proper representation and a speedy trial." Since it is difficult to imagine a legal-aid society strike which did not have these consequences, the affirmative answer to the question by the County Lawyers' Association seems theoretical at best.[55] The Association's opinion was subsequently criticized.[56]

NOTES

1. NAACP v. Button, 371 U.S. 415 (1963).
2. United Transp. Union v. State Bar of Mich., 401 U.S. 576, 585–86 (1971). *See also* Brotherhood of Railroad Trainmen v. Virginia State Bar, 377 U.S. 1 (1964); United Mine Workers v. Illinois Bar Ass'n, 389 U.S. 217 (1967).

Cf. Boddie v. Connecticut, 401 U.S. 371 (1971) (holding that an indigent has a constitutional right of access to a state's divorce courts even if she cannot afford to pay the filing fees).

3. *See, e.g.,* Feinstein v. Attorney General, 36 N.Y.2d 199, 326 N.E.2d 288, 366 N.Y.S.2d 613, (1975).
4. Hooper v. City of Madison, 79 Wisc.2d 120, 256 N.W.2d 139 (1977).
5. Canon 7 and Disciplinary Rule 7-102(A), Code of Professional Responsibility, ABA. See Drago v. Buonagurio, —— N.Y.2d ——, —— N.Y.S.2d ——, —— N.E.2d —— (Dec. 20, 1978) (holding a lawyer not liable to a defendant against whom he filed a law suit without foundation).
6. Acevedo v. Immigration and Naturalization Service, 538 F.2d 918, 919, 921 (2d Cir. 1976). *See also* Katris v. I.N.S., 562 F.2d 866 (2d Cir. 1977).
7. Disciplinary Rule 7-102(B), Code of Professional Responsibility, ABA.
8. Disciplinary Rule 7-102(B), Code of Professional Responsibility, ABA, as amended March 1, 1974. Opinions 287 & 341, ABA.
9. *In re* A., 276 Or. 225, 554 P.2d 479 (1976).
10. *See* Freedman, Lawyers' Ethics in an Adversary System (1975).
11. Overmeyer v. Fidelity and Deposit Co. of Md., 554 F.2d 539 (2d Cir. 1977). *Cf. in re* Sutter, 543 F.2d 1030 (2d Cir. 1976) (lawyer fined for failure to appear in court on day set for trial, despite assertion he was then defending another client in another court).
12. Opinion 337, ABA (Aug. 10, 1974).
13. Maness v. Meyers, 419 U.S. 449, 465, 466, 467 (1975).
14. Disciplinary Rule 5-101, Code of Professional Responsibility, ABA.
15. Disciplinary Rule 5-102, Code of Professional Responsibility, ABA; *in re* Rappaport, 558 F.2d 87, 91 (2d cir. 1977).
16. J.P. Foley & Co. v. Vanderbilt, 523 F.2d 1357 (2d Cir. 1975); *in re* Wertman Estate, 462 Pa. 195, 340 A.2d 429 (1975); Watson v. Alford, 255 Ark. 911, 503 S.W.2d 897 (1974); Sheldon Elec. Co. v. Blackhawk Htg. & Plbg. Co., 423 F. Supp. 486 (S.D.N.Y. 1976).
17. Disciplinary Rule 7-102(A)(2), Code of Professional Responsibility, ABA.
18. *In re* Bithoney, 486 F.2d 319 (1st Cir. 1973). *See also* Drago, *supra* note 5.
19. L.W. Holt v. Commonwealth of Virginia, 381 U.S. 131, 133, 137 (1965).

20. United States v. Meyer, 346 F. Supp. 973, 978 (D.D.C. 1972).
21. *Ibid.*, at 973; United States v. Seale, 461 F.2d 345 (7th Cir. 1972); *in re* Brown, 454 F.2d 999, 1005 (D.C. Cir. 1971).
22. United States v. Meyer, *supra* note 20, at 973, 978–79.
23. United States v. Seale, *supra* note 21, at 345, 370.
24. *In re* Little, 404 U.S. 553, 555 (1972), quoting from Craig v. Harney, 331 U.S. 367, 376, 376 (1947) and Brown v. United States, 356 U.S. 148, 153 (1958).
25. *In re* Buckley, 10 Cal.3d 237, 243, 248, 250, 514 P.2d 1201, 1204, 1207–9, 110 Cal. Rptr. 121, 124, 127–29, 68 A.L.R.3d 248 (1973), *cert. denied*, 418 U.S. 910 (1974).
26. *See, generally,* Annot., Attorney's Addressing Allegedly Insulting Remarks to Court During the Course of Trial as Contempt, 68 A.L.R.3d 273-302 (1976). *See also* Annot., Conduct of Attorney in Connection with Making Objections or Taking Exceptions as Contempt of Court, 68 A.L.R.3d 314–53 (1976).
27. State v. Nelson, 210 Kan. 637, 638, 642, 504 P.2d 211, 213, 216 (1972).
28. *In re* Justices of the App. Div., 33 N.Y.2d 559, 301 N.E.2d 426, 347 N.Y.S.2d 441 (1973). *See also* Polk v. State Bar of Tex., 374 F. Supp. 784 (N.D. Tex. 1974).
29. *In re* Raggio, 87 Nev. 369, 487 P.2d 499 (1971). *See also in re* Whiteside, 386 F.2d 805 (2d Cir. 1967), *cert. denied*, 391 U.S. 920 (1968) (disbarment justified where attorney filed lawsuit charging state trial and appellate judges with participation in criminal conspiracy when he had no evidence to support charge); Eisenberg v. Boardman, 302 F. Supp. 1360 (W.D. Wis. 1969).
30. *In re* Sawyer, 360 U.S. 622 (1959).
31. Polk, *supra* note 28; State Bar of Tex. v. Semaan, 508 S.W.2d 429 (Tex. Civ. App. 1974); Eisenberg, *supra* note 29.
32. State v. Nelson, 210 Kan. 637, 504 P.2d 211 (1972). *In re* Justices of the App. Div., 33 N.Y.2d 559, 347 N.Y.S.2d 441, 301 N.E.2d 426 (1973). *See, generally,* Annot., Attorney's Criticism of Judicial Acts as Ground of Disciplinary Action, 12 A.L.R.3d 1408–42 (1967).
33. Nebraska Press Ass'n v. Stuart, 427 U.S. 539 (1976).
34. Rosato v. Superior Ct. of Fresno County, 51 Cal. App. 3d 190, 124 Cal. Rptr. 427 (1975), *cert. denied*, 427 U.S. 912 (1976).
35. Chicago Council of Lawyers v. Bauer, 522 F.2d 242, 249 (7th Cir. 1975), *cert. denied*, 427 U.S. 912 (1976).
36. Farr v. Pitchess, 522 F.2d 464 (9th Cir. 1975), *cert. de-*

nied, 427 U.S. 912 (1976). People v. Dupree, 88 Misc. 2d 780, 388 N.Y.S.2d 203 (Sup Ct. New York County 1976).
37. Markfield v. Association of the Bar of the City of N.Y., 49 App. Div. 2d 516, 517, 370 N.Y.S.2d 82, 85 (1st Dept. 1975).
38. In re Connelly, 18 App. Div. 2d 466, 240 N.Y.S.2d 126 (1st Dept. 1963).
39. Opinion 439, New York State Bar Ass'n (July 23, 1976). See also Opinion 449, New York State Bar Ass'n (December 13, 1976), stating that it is not unethical for a lawyer to advertise in a bar journal for other lawyers representing other litigants in similar actions under certain circumstances.
40. Bates v. State Bar of Arizona, 433 U.S. 350 (1977). One post-Bates case has rejected a First Amendment right of law firm associates going off on their own to send announcements to the firm's active clients encouraging the clients to go with them. Adler, Barish, Daniels, Levin & Creskoff v. Epstein, 47 L.W. 2246 (Pa. Sup. Ct. Oct. 24, 1978). See also in re Petition for rule of court governing lawyer advertising, —— Tenn. ——, 504 S.W.2d 638 (1978) for a state supreme court's reaction to Bates.
41. Belli v. State Bar of Cal., 10 Cal.3d 824, 519 P.2d 575, 112 Cal. Rptr. 527 (1974).
42. Jacoby v. State Bar of Cal., 19 Cal.3d 359, 562 P.2d 1326, 138 Cal. Rptr. 77 (1977). This "revision" of the "public's right to know" is no doubt a salutory development, but it can work "retroactive" hardship. In 1963, four partners in a New York law firm were censured because they cooperated with Life magazine in an article entitled "Behind the Scenes Tour of Today's Legal Labyrinths: Lawyers Who Try Not to Try Cases." It is unlikely, after the Bates and Jacoby cases, that censure would still be applied in that case today. There is a lesson to be learned in the fact that conduct which today is considered in the vanguard was, a mere decade and a half ago, considered "unethical, improper, unjustified and dishonorable." In re Connelly, supra note 38.
43. See 63 A.B.A.J. 1234 (September 1977).
44. N.Y.L.J., Nov. 4, 1977, p. 1.
45. In re Madsen, —— Ill.2d ——, —— N.E.2d —— (1977).
46. Coles v. Marsh, 560 F.2d 186 (3d Cir. 1977), cert denied, 434 U.S. 905 (1977).
47. Ohralik v. Ohio State Bar Ass'n, 436 U.S. 44 (1978).
48. In re Primus, 436 U.S. 412 (1978).
49. A good article on solicitation appears in the October 11, 1977 issue of the Los Angeles Times, p. 1.

50. La Rocca v. Lane, 37 N.Y.2d 575, 582, 338 N.E.2d 606, 612, 376 N.Y.S.2d 93, 100 (1975), *cert. denied*, 424 U.S. 968 (1976).
51. Sandstrom v. State, 309 So.2d 17, 19 (Dist. Ct. App. Fla. 1975). (There is some indication in this opinion that the reviewing court was offended because the lawyer forced the judge into a contempt situation rather than seeking collateral review of his order.)
52. Peck v. Stone, 32 App. Div. 2d 506, 507, 508, 304 N.Y.S.2d 881, 883, 884 (4th Dept. 1969).
53. *In re* De Carlo, 141 N.J. Super. 42, 47, 357 A.2d 273, 275 (1976).
54. Kersevich v. Jaffrey Dist. Ct., 114 N.H. 790, 330 A.2d 446, 448 (1974). Close-It Enterprises, Inc. v. Weinberger, —— App. Div. 2d ——, —— N.Y.S.2d —— (2nd Dept. 1978).
55. Question 645, New York County Lawyers' Ass'n Comm. on Professional Ethics (N.Y.L.J., June 9, 1975, p. 3).
56. Freedman, *The Legal Aid Strike*, N.Y.L.J., June 25, 1975, p.1, for criticism of the Opinion.

X

The Rights of Indigents, Clients Who Represent Themselves, and Nonlawyers Who Sell Law-Related Services

Can a person who is not an attorney represent herself in court?

Generally, yes. If the person is a defendant in a criminal case, she has a constitutional right to represent herself under the Sixth Amendment, although it would be foolish in all but the most petty cases.[1] The Sixth Amendment right also applies to state criminal trials.[2] The United States and many states have rules allowing a person to represent herself, either as plaintiff or defendant, in a civil proceeding.[3] Often, however, this right does not apply if a nonlawyer is seeking to represent a corporation, even if it is a small corporation in which she is the only stockholder. In such circumstances, the litigant must have an attorney represent the corporation.[4] This is because the corporation is seen as a separate entity and a nonlawyer, while entitled to represent his or her own interests, cannot represent the interests of another. But a nonlawyer can generally represent a partnership in which he or she has an interest, because the partnership, unlike a corporation, is not considered a separate entity.[5] A nonlawyer may never represent another person in court no matter how knowledgeable the nonlawyer may be about the law, even if the nonlawyer has gone to law school but is not a member of the bar. Such representation is considered the practice of law without a license and is criminal.[6]

What is the "unauthorized practice of law"?

This varies from state to state. Generally, the courts of a state have the power to define what the practice of law is. The purpose of prohibiting the unauthorized practice of law is to protect the public from persons who have not demonstrated their competence and fitness to practice law. There is no detailed list of acts which only lawyers can do. The fact that a layman does not take compensation for giving legal advice is not a defense to a charge of the unauthorized practice of law.[7] On the other hand, nonlawyers are often permitted to fill many of the same functions for which people retain lawyers.

Although the definition of the "practice of law" necessarily depends upon the particular facts of each case, the New Mexico Supreme Court recently provided a fairly complete, though still general, list. It said that the

> indicia of the practice of law, insofar as court proceedings are concerned, include the following: (1) representation of parties before judicial or administrative bodies, (2) preparation of pleadings and other papers incident to actions and special proceedings, (3) management of such action and proceeding; and non-court-related activities such as (4) giving legal advice and counsel, (5) rendering a service that requires the use of legal knowledge or skill, (6) preparing instruments and contracts by which legal rights are secured.[8]

Doesn't this mean that lawyers can maintain a monopoly on a lot of different services, which could easily be done by nonlawyers, simply by calling the service the "practice of law"?

Yes, and the laymen and consumer groups are beginning to realize that. Even courts are becoming more sensitive to the problem. For example, the New York County Lawyers' Association charged that the book *How to Avoid*

Probate, by Norman Dacey, amounted to the practice of law without a license. Dacey was not an attorney. The book was a legal text which purported to tell readers what the law was with regard to the distribution of a person's property after death. The book contained many forms for different legal situations and the text described how to complete the forms. The New York Court of Appeals, reversing a lower-court decision, ruled that the sale of the book did not constitute the unauthorized practice of law.[9] Subsequently, Dacey sued in federal court for damages, but the case was thrown out on the ground that the bar association, although wrong in its belief, had probable cause to believe that the book was illegal.[10]

What about "divorce-yourself" kits? Are these permitted?

It depends on the state you're in. In New York, an intermediate appellate court has held that the publication and sale of a "divorce-yourself" kit, aimed at couples who wish to obtain uncontested divorces in the New York courts, does not amount to the unlawful practice of law. Nor could the publisher be enjoined from maintaining an office for purposes of selling the kit to buyers. But the court also found that the publisher of the kit had engaged in the unauthorized practice of law by giving "legal advice in the course of personal contacts concerning particular problems which might arise in the preparation and presentation of the purchaser's asserted matrimonial cause of action or pursuit of other legal remedies and assistance in the preparation of necessary documents." In other words, it was all right to sell the kits, but it was illegal to advise purchasers about their particular situation.[11] The Oregon Supreme Court agreed in a similar case a few years later.[12] The Florida Supreme Court, however, took the opposite point of view.[13]

If a litigant who is not a lawyer represents himself, will he get any special benefit?

In most states, he will not. He will be charged with knowledge of the law and the rules of the court.[14] He assumes responsibility for his own inadequacy and lack of knowledge about the procedural and substantive law.[15] He assumes the same standards for honesty and good faith imposed upon an attorney.[16] On the other hand, some courts do say that a layman who represents himself will not be held to the same standards of skill and judgment which must be attributed to an attorney.[17]

Does a person who is unable to afford counsel have a constitutional right to a lawyer?

Only in a criminal proceeding which can result in incarceration.[18] A civil litigant, whether he is a plaintiff or a defendant, does not have a constitutional right to the appointment of free counsel. Still, the federal government and some states have provisions under which an indigent may have a statutory right to counsel in a court's discretion.[19]

Does an indigent criminal defendant have the right to have a particular attorney appointed to represent him?

No. Although the court may accede to that request, particularly if the lawyer is willing to be appointed, it does not have to do so. The decision is in the court's discretion and so long as it does not abuse its discretion in appointing counsel, the defendant has to accept the lawyer assigned to him.

In one leading case, decided recently by the California Supreme Court, the defendant was on trial for murder. An attorney with substantial experience in trying murder cases, and one whom the defendant wished to have appointed to represent him, agreed to the appointment. Nevertheless, the trial judge declined to appoint that attorney and instead appointed a different lawyer. On review in the Supreme Court of California, a five-to-two majority of the court held that this was not error. No constitutional or statutory guarantee was violated "by the appointment of an attorney other than the one requested by defendant. . . . The additional factor that requested counsel has indicated his willingness and availability to act does not raise any constitutional compulsion requiring his appointment." The two dissenting justices could not understand how the administration of justice was served by the refusal to allow the defendant to have counsel of his choosing. The dissenters also emphasized that "effective advocacy involves more than vigor, experience and familiarity with the law. The attorney-client relationship contemplates trust and mutual cooperation...." The dissenters rejected the "implication in these proceedings that because defendant is indigent and counsel is appointed, the need for trust and confidence between attorney and client is somewhat less significant."[20]

The overwhelming majority of the cases follow the principle that the indigent client is not entitled to select his counsel.[21] There may be an exception when an out-of-state lawyer seeks to be appointed as co-counsel with a local appointed lawyer to represent an indigent defendant and waives any right he might have to a fee from the state.[22]

What if an indigent defendant simply cannot get along with his appointed counsel?

He can make a motion for a change of counsel, or request his lawyer to do so, and the trial judge will have to decide whether to grant the motion. The defendant will have to show a good reason, such as that his lawyer has a conflict of interest or there has been a complete breakdown in communication between the lawyer and the accused. The trial court's decision on the motion will be final, unless it is an abuse of discretion.[23]

Is it possible to have an attorney-client relationship even if the client is not paying the attorney?

Definitely. And this is true whether or not the attorney has been appointed by the court to represent the client.[24]

Does the attorney-client relationship apply even if the attorney is assigned by the court to represent the client and the state pays his fee?

Absolutely. It doesn't matter if the attorney is assigned by the state or is provided by a legal-aid society. In either event, the attorney-client relationship exists with the same force as if the client had paid to retain the attorney.[25]

But doesn't a lawyer who is paid by the state to represent an indigent defendant have a loyalty to the people who are paying her?

No. As one federal appellate court wrote:

Whether a lawyer is employed by a prosperous defendant at a handsome fee or serves an indigent without compensation in the discharge of the duty resting upon him as an officer of the court, the canons of our profession require his "entire devotion to the interest of the client, warm zeal in the maintenance and defense of his rights, and the exertion of his utmost learning and ability."[26]

NOTES

1. United States v. Jones, 514 F.2d 1331 (D.C. Cir. 1975).
2. Faretta v. California, 422 U.S. 806 (1975).
3. 28 U.S.C. § 1654 (1966); Dobbins v. Dobbins, 234 Ga. 347, 216 S.E.2d 102 (1975), cert. denied, 423 U.S. 1019 (1975); Heikes v. Fort Collins Prod. Cred. Ass'n, 169 Colo. 27, 456 P.2d 274 (1969); in re Ellis, 53 Haw. 23, 487 P.2d 286 (1971), cert. denied, 405 U.S. 1075 (1972).
4. Simbraw, Inc. v. United States, 367 F.2d 373 (3rd Cir. 1966).
5. United States v. Reeves, 431 F.2d 1187 (9th Cir. 1970).
6. N.Y. JUD. LAW § 476-a, 476-b, and 476-c (McKinney). But cf. Oregon State Bar Assoc. v. Wright, —— Ore. ——, 573 P.2d 283 (1977).
7. Darby v. Mississippi Bd. of Bar Admissions, 185 So.2d 684 (Miss. 1966).
8. Norvell v. Credit Bur. of Albuquerque, Inc., 85 N.M. 521, 514 P.2d 40 (1973). See another New Mexico case for an example of the effort of that state's bar association to protect its economic interests. State Bar v. Guardian Abstract & Title Co., 91 N.M. 434, 575 P.2d 943 (1978).
9. New York County Lawyers' Ass'n v. Dacey, 21 N.Y.2d 694, 234 N.E.2d 459, 287 N.Y.S.2d 422 (1967).
10. Dacey v. New York County Lawyers' Ass'n, 423 F.2d 188 (2d Cir. 1969), cert. denied, 398 U.S. 929 (1970).
11. State v. Winder, 42 App. Div. 2d 1039, 348 N.Y.S.2d 270 (4th Dept. 1973).
12. Oregon Bar v. Gilchrist, 272 Or. 552, 538 P.2d 913 (1975).
13. Florida Bar v. Stupica, 300 So. 2d 683 (Fla. 1974).
14. Bettum v. Montgomery Fed. Svgs. & Loan Ass'n, 262 Md. 360, 277 A.2d 600 (1971).

THE RIGHTS OF INDIGENTS

15. Marchand v. Gene Thorpe Fin., Inc., 225 So.2d 485 (La. App. 1969).
16. Gajewski v. Bratcher, 240 N.W.2d 871 (N.D. 1976).
17. Connolly v. Connolly, 316 So.2d 167 (La. App. 1975).
18. Argersinger v. Hamlin, 407 U.S. 25 (1972); Douglas v. California, 372 U.S. 353 (1963).
19. *In re* Smiley, 36 NY.2d 433, 330 N.E.2d 53, 369 N.Y.S.2d 87 (1975). United States v. McQuade, 579 F.2d 1180 (9th Cir. 1978). Gordon v. Leeke, 574 F.2d 1147 (4th Cir. 1978).
20. Drumgo v. Superior Ct. of Marin County, 8 Cal.3d 930, 938-39, 506 P.2d 1007, 1012-13, 106 Cal. Rptr. 631, 636–37 (1973), *cert. denied*, 414 U.S. 979 (1973).
21. People v. Cox, 22 Ill.2d 534, 177 N.E.2d 211 (1961), *cert. denied*, 374 U.S. 855 (1963); Lepiscopo v. United States, 469 F.2d 650 (5th Cir. 1972); People v. Ginther, 390 Mich. 436, 212 N.W.2d 922 (1973).
22. Magee v. Superior Court San Francisco, 8 Cal.3d 949, 506 P.2d 1023, 106 Cal. Rptr. 647 (1973).
23. United States v. Calabro, 467 F.2d 973 (2d Cir. 1972), *cert. denied*, 410 U.S. 926 (1973); People v. Ginther, *supra* note 21.
24. Fort Myers Seafood Packers, Inc. v. Steptoe and Johnson, 381 F.2d 261 (D.C. Cir. 1967), *cert. denied*, 390 U.S. 946 (1968).
25. Young v. United States, 346 F.2d 793 (D.C. Cir. 1965); Turner v. Maryland, 318 F.2d 852 (4th Cir. 1963).
26. Turner, *supra* note 25, at 852, 854. *Cf.* People v. Aiken, 45 N.Y.2d 394, 408 N.Y.S.2d 444, —— N.E.2d —— (1978).

Appendix A
State Bar Admission and Reciprocity

The following pages list, for each state, the (1) address to which you should write for detailed information on the state's bar admission requirement; (2) whether the state has a residency requirement for its examination or admission to its bar; and (3) the state's reciprocity rules, if any.

This is intended to be a summary only; you should write for the particular state's rules before relying on the information in this appendix. First, rules may have changed since this summary was completed. Second, many state rules contain abundant detail; obviously, only the broad outlines could be summarized. Reference to the rules themselves will be necessary to see if any of the nuances affect your particular situation. Finally, if you have a particular question not apparent on the face of the rules, inquire in writing. The answer may be a matter of interpretation. For example, a state that requires five years of practice in order to admit a lawyer on the basis of reciprocity may recognize full-time law teaching as "practice" even though its rules don't say so.

Alabama

Alabama State Bar Board of Examiners
P.O. Box 671
Montgomery, Ala. 36101
(205) 269-1515

Must be a bona-fide resident at time of application. Must be actual resident at time of certification.

Examination required by all except those who taught at an accredited Alabama Law School for three consecutive years and who are residents.

Alaska

Alaska Bar Association
P.O. Box 279
Anchorage, Alaska 99510
(907) 272-7469

Must be bona-fide resident for thirty days prior to exam and continuing through admission.

Attorneys who have practiced for five of the seven years immediately preceeding exam may be eligible for the one day attorney exam.

Arizona

Committee on Character and Fitness
Suite 858, 234 North Central Ave.,
Phoenix, Ariz. 85004
(602) 252-4804

No residency requirements.

Examination required of all applicants.

Arkansas

State Board of Law Examiners
P.O. Box 5133
Little Rock, Ark. 72205
(501) 633-4619

Must be resident for sixty days prior to application. Waivable.

May be admitted without exam if member of Bar in another jurisdiction for at least four years and engaged in active practice of law for at least three years immediately preceding application. Must also be resident. Waiver of three-year-practice rule may be granted for veterans.

California

The Committee of Bar Examiners of the State Bar of California
Rm. 501, 633 Battery St.
San Francisco, Calif. 94111
(415) 982-6626
1230 West Third St.
Los Angeles, Calif. 90017
(213) 482-4040

No residency requirements.

Examination required. Attorneys who have practiced in a U.S. jurisdiction four out of the immediately preceding six years may be eligible for attorney exam. Provision for admission of foreign lawyers from both common-law and non-common-law jurisdictions.

Colorado
Colorado State Board of Law Examiners
Colorado State Judicial Building
Rm. 470, 2 East 14th Ave.
Denver, Colo. 80203
(303) 861-1111

Must be a bona-fide resident beginning thirty days prior to the commencement of the bar examination and continuing through admission. Practitioners from states other than those admitted without examinations may take the examination upon representation that they intend to become residents after passing the exam, but they may be admitted only after actually becoming residents, and this must occur within six months of passing.

Practitioners from other states who have taught or practiced law for eight out of the prior ten years and who, when admitted, had attained qualifications at least equal to those then required for admission by examination to Colorado can be admitted without examination, but must become Colorado residents within six months after admission. Practitioners who have practiced eighteen out of the prior twenty-five years may be admitted even if at the time of their admission they had not attained qualifications equal to those then required for admission by examination to Colorado.

Connecticut
Connecticut Bar Examining Committee
Henry B. Anderson, Secretary
P.O. Box 1109
New Milford, Conn. 06776
(203) 354-3987

Applicant must be a resident of Connecticut or intend to become a resident of the State.

May be admitted without examination. Must have practiced for at least five years immediately preceding application. Must be actual resident for six months immediately preceding admission. Must have practiced for ten years immediately preceding application if previously failed Connecticut bar examination.

Delaware
Board of Bar Examiners of the State of Delaware

P.O. Box 8965
Wilmington, Del. 19899
(302) 571-6728

Applicant must be a bona-fide resident at time of examination, and must reside in Delaware for five months before being admitted to the bar.

Examination required of all applicants, although special attorney exam may be given to those who have practiced in another jurisdiction for five years preceding application. Must be a resident of the state of Delaware when applying, with no intention of moving.

District of Columbia
Committee on Admissions
D.C. Court of Appeals
Rm. 311-A, 400 F Street, N.W.
Washington, D.C. 20001
(202) 727-1806

No residency requirements.

May be admitted without examination. Must have practiced for five years of the eight years immediately preceding application. Time requirement may be shortened under certain circumstances.

Florida
Florida Board of Bar Examiners
1300 East Park Ave.
Tallahassee, Fla. 32301

No residency requirements.

Examination required of all applicants.

Georgia
Office of Bar Admissions
610 State Judicial Building
Atlanta, Ga. 30334
(404) 656-3490

No residency requirement to take exam.

Exam required of all.

Hawaii
Board of Examiners
Supreme Court of Hawaii
P.O. Box 2560
Honolulu, Hawaii 96804
(808) 548-7431

No person shall be admitted unless applicant is and will have been continuously an actual and bona-fide resident of the state of Hawaii for three months immediately prior to being admitted and shall have been physically present within the state of Hawaii for at least 75 percent of the said three-month period.

Examination required of all applicants, except certain faculty members at the University of Hawaii.

Idaho
Board of Commissioners of the Idaho State Bar
P.O. Box 895
Boise, Idaho 83701
(208) 342-8958

Affidavit of intent to reside in Idaho must be filed at time of application. Resident at admission.

Attorneys from other states who have practiced five out of the last seven years take a two-day essay examination, and not the multistate examination. All others must take the full examination.

Illinois
State Board of Law Examiners
Attention: John B. Hendricks
412 Ridgely Building
Springfield, Ill. 62701

No residence requirement to take exam.

Lawyers who have practiced for five of the prior seven years and who have the educational qualifications required of applicants to the examination may be admitted on motion. No applicant may be admitted on motion on terms more favorable than the applicant's state provides to Illinois attorneys. Must be actual resident of the State of Illinois at the time of application.

Indiana
State Board of Law Examiners
402 State House
Indianapolis, Ind. 46204
(317) 633-6704

Must be bona-fide resident and submit affidavit of intent to engage in practice of law in Indiana within two years after admission.

Examination required of applicants from jurisdictions requiring examination of Indiana applicants. Must be bona-fide resident of Indiana (some exceptions). Must have practiced five to seven years immediately preceding application. Provision for common-law lawyers.

Iowa
Board of Law Examiners
State Capitol Building
Des Moines, Iowa 50319
(515) 281-5911

Must be inhabitant of Iowa.

May be admitted without examination. Must be resident and have practiced or taught law five to seven years immediately preceding application.

Kansas
The Clerk of Supreme Court
Statehouse
Topeka, Kans. 66612
(913) 296-3229

Must be a resident at time of application.

May be admitted without examination if applicant is or will be bona-fide resident of Kansas prior to the time he is admitted to the bar of Kansas and if at the time was first admitted in another jurisdiction was fully qualified to have taken the bar examination in Kansas under the rules of this Court then in effect. Applicant must have practiced continuously in the jurisdiction in which applicant was duly admitted for a period of five years and must have continued to practice there and elsewhere until within six months of making application for admission here.

Kentucky
Kentucky State Board of Bar Examiners
716 Lexington Building
201-215 West Short St.
Lexington, Ky. 40507
(606) 253-2733

For examination, must be permanent resident, or graduate from approved law school in Kentucky, or intend to become resident or perform major portion of practice in Kentucky. For admission without examination, must have been resident continuously for ninety-day period preceding admission and intend to reside permanently, or prove genuine intent to perform major portion of practice in Kentucky.

A lawyer who has been engaged in the active practice of the law in another state for five of the seven years preceding application may be admitted to the bar of this state without examination provided that the qualifications required for admission to the bar in such district or state were, at the time of admission, equal to or higher than those for admission to the bar examination in the state of Kentucky at that time. Active engagement in the teaching of the law shall be considered active engagement in the practice of the law.

Louisiana
Supreme Court of Louisiana Committee on Bar Admissions
Suite 210, 225 Baronne St.
New Orleans, La. 70112
(504) 566-1600

APPENDIX A

No residency requirements.

Examination required of all applicants.

Maine
Sumner T. Bernstein, Secretary
Maine Board of Bar Examiners
One Monument Square
Portland, Maine 04111
(207) 774-6291

No residency requirements for examination, but residence (domicile) is required for admission.

Examination required of all applicants but shortened examinations possible for some who have taken multistate bar exam.

Maryland
Maryland State Board of Law Examiners
93 Main St., Fourth Floor
Annapolis, Md. 21401

Must be domiciled at time of application and at admission.

May be admitted on attorney's examination. Must be domiciled in Maryland at the time of application, state intent to practice in Maryland, and have practiced or taught law five of seven years preceding application. Out-of-state attorneys are required to take a three-hour essay examination on Maryland Rules of Practice and Procedure.

Massachusetts
Board of Bar Examiners
77 Franklin St.
Boston, Mass. 02100
(617) 482-4466

Office of the Clerk Supreme Judicial Court
New Court House
Pemberton Square
Boston, Mass. 02110

No residency requirements for admission by examination.

May be admitted without examination. Must have been admitted at least five years in other jurisdiction and have practiced or taught law for unspecified length of time. Residence in Massachusetts necessary at time of application. Provision for foreign lawyers.

Michigan
Board of Law Examiners
306 Townsend St.
Lansing, Mich. 48909
(517) 373 0119

No residency requirements for admission by examination. Must be a resident at time of admission for admission by reciprocity.

Must have taught or practiced law three out of last five years. Must be a resident of Michigan and intend to make practice of law in Michigan principal occupation.

Minnesota
State Board of Law Examiners
Suite 200-A, 200 South Robert St.
St. Paul, Minn. 55107
(612) 222-2050

Resident, or office in state, or if not a resident, must appoint Clerk of Supreme Court agent for service of process.

May be admitted without examination. Must have practiced for at least five of seven years preceding admission. Provision for admission of legal-service lawyers.

Mississippi
Board of Bar Admissions
620 North State St.
Jackson, Miss. 39201
(601) 354-7480

Must be resident at time of making application.

May be admitted without examination from states with equivalent requirements granting similar privileges to applicants from Mississippi. Must be a resident at least six months prior to making application and have practiced five years.

Missouri
Clerk of the Supreme Court
Jefferson City, Mo. 65101
(314) 751-4144

Must be bona-fide resident for admission; or be resident of adjoining county in adjacent state with intent to maintain office and practice law full time in Missouri.

May be admitted without examination. Must have practiced or taught law for at least five years immediately preceding application. Same residency requirement as for admission by examination.

Montana
Clerk of the Supreme Court
Montana State Board of Law Examiners
Capitol Building
Helena, Mont. 59601
(406) 499-2470

Must be resident at least six months prior to making application.

May be admitted without examination. Must have practiced for at least two years immediately preceding application. Same residency requirements as admission by examination.

Nebraska
Nebraska State Bar Commission
2413 State Capitol Building

Lincoln, Nebr. 68509
(402) 432-4447

Applicant must be a resident at time application is filed.

May be admitted without examination. Must be a resident at time of application and either have five years practice out of prior ten, or have qualifications, at time of admission to other jurisdiction, equal to those required at present for Nebraska admission.

Nevada
Board of Bar Examiners,
State Bar of Nevada
P.O. Box 2125
Reno, Nev. 89505
(702) 323-0338

Must be resident as of March 1.

Examination required of all applicants, except some law teachers.

New Hampshire
Office of the Clerk
New Hampshire Supreme Court
Supreme Court Building
Concord, N.H. 03301
(603) 271-2646

Must be a resident at the time of admission; not necessary at time of examination.

May be admitted without examination from state having equal standards of admission. Must be bona-fide resident and have practiced five years preceding time of application.

New Jersey
Board of Bar Examiners
State House Annex, Room 432
P.O. Box 1480
Trenton, N.J. 08625
(609) 292-4837

No residency requirements for examination, provided that within thirty days after taking attorneys' oath, attorney becomes domiciled or establishes principal office for practice of law in New Jersey.

Examination required of all applicants except qualified law professors. Certain exceptions for legal-services lawyers.

New Mexico
Secretary
Board of Examiners
P.O. Box 848
Santa Fe, N. Mex. 87503
(505) 827-2412

Must be resident at least ninety days prior to admission (physically present for seventy-five days).

Examination required of all applicants. Law faculty of the University of New Mexico may be admitted without examination. Attorneys who have practiced for 5 of 6 years immediately preceding application may be eligible for special attorney's examination. There are rules permitting the admission of law teachers without examination under certain conditions.

New York
New York State Board of Law Examiners
90 State St.
Albany, N.Y. 12207
(518) 463-2841

To take the exam an applicant must either be a resident of or employed full time in the state, or intend in good faith to commence employment or establish residence within two months after exam. Must complete six months residence or employment prior to being certified for admission.

May be admitted without examination from every jurisdiction. Must be resident at least six months prior to application and have practiced five years preceding application. May be admitted from some foreign countries. Additional special rules for law teachers and legal-services lawyers.

North Carolina
Board of Law Examiners of the State of North Carolina
107 Fayetteville St.
P.O. Box 25427
Raleigh, N.C. 27611
(919) 828-4886

Must be resident by June 15th of the year the applicant takes the exam.

May be admitted without examination from states admitting attorneys from North Carolina without examination. Must be resident sixty days prior to consideration of application, and have practiced or taught law at an approved school three of the five years immediately preceding filing of application.

North Dakota
Luella Dunn
Clerk of the Supreme Court
State Capitol
Bismarck, N. Dak. 58505
(701) 224-2221

Need not be resident to participate in bar exam; however, residency is a prerequisite for admission.

Shall have taught or practiced law for at least four of prior five years.

Ohio
Ohio Board of Bar Examiners
Supreme Court of Ohio
30 East Broad St.
Columbus, Ohio 43215
(614) 466-4533

None; however, residency required for admission without examination.

May be admitted without examination. Must be a resident at time of admission, have practiced or taught law for at least five years, and not have failed Ohio Bar Exam.

Oklahoma
Board of Bar Examiners
P.O. Box 53036
1901 North Lincoln Boulevard
Oklahoma City, Okla. 73105
(405) 524-2365

Must be resident at time of admission.

May be admitted without examination. Examination required of applicants from jurisdictions requiring examination of Oklahoma applicants. Must have practiced for five years immediately preceding application and be a resident at time of admission.

Oregon
Board of Bar Examiners
1776 W. Madison St.
Portland, Oreg. 97205
(503) 229-5788

Must be a resident at the time of admission.

Examination required of all applicants, although attorneys who have practiced three of the five preceding years may be eligible for an attorney exam. Must be resident at time of admission. Recognizes attorneys from other common-law countries.

Pennsylvania
State Board of Law Examiners
2010 Two Girard Plaza
Philadelphia, Pa. 19102
(215) 564-1724

Must certify to address in commonwealth where paper may be served.

May be admitted without examination. Must have taught law or practiced for at least five years outside of the commonwealth in a state granting reciprocity to Pennsylvanians. Provision for admission of foreign lawyers. Provision for legal-services lawyers.

Rhode Island
Rhode Island Board of Bar Examiners
Rhode Island Supreme Court
250 Benefit St.
Providence, R.I. 02903
(401) 331-0132

Must intend to practice law in the state.

Five years' active practice in another jurisdiction out of the prior ten years and three months' residency.

South Carolina

South Carolina State Board of Law Examiners
P.O. Box 11330
Columbia, S.C. 29211
803-758-3741

Must be a bona-fide resident, continuously, from April 1 or November 1 prior to the July or February examination, respectively.

Examination required of all applicants; certain exceptions for law teachers.

South Dakota

State Board of Bar Examiners
Capitol Building
Pierre, S. Dak. 57501
(605) 224-3511

Must be resident at time of admission.

May be admitted without examination. Must have practiced five years preceding application and be a resident at time of admission. Military legal experience and law teaching apply toward five-year rule.

Tennessee

Board of Law Examiners of Tennessee
415 Supreme Court Building
Nashville, Tenn. 37219
(615) 741-3234

Must intend to reside and actively engage in the practice of law in Tennessee before being eligible to take exam. Must establish physical residence and domicile in Tennessee for a period of at least two months before being eligible to receive license if successful on examination.

No exam necessary if engaged in practice for five years in a state which grants similar privilege to applicants from Tennessee. Must be resident for two months prior to admission and meet other requirements of Rule 37. Possibility of admission of out-of-state lawyers who have practiced fewer than five years under certain conditions.

Texas

State Board of Law Examiners
Fifth Floor, Texas Law Center
P.O. Box 12248
Capitol Station
Austin, Tex. 78711
(512) 475-4235

Must be a resident for a minimum of three months preceding examination.

Will be considered for admission without examination if graduate of law school approved by Texas Supreme Court and ABA, with at least seven years' practice satisfactory to board preceding removal to Texas; ten years' practice required if not graduate of approved law school. Attorney must also show that the state from which such attorney emigrates to Texas grants reciprocal privileges to Texas attorneys with such length of practice and educational background. Teaching is considered to be practice.

Utah

Utah State Bar
Office of the Executive Director
425 East First South
Salt La. City, Utah 84111

There is a three month residency requirement before attorneys or law graduates may take the bar exam.

Reciprocity granted to same extent that Utah lawyers receive from the sister state. Applicant must also have practiced for three of the last five years.

Vermont

Supreme Court
111 State St.
Montpelier, Vt. 05602
(802) 828-3281

Must be resident six months prior to admission.

May be admitted without examination. Must have engaged in active practice for five of the ten years immediately preceding application. Must have six months' residency and six months of clerkship under a Vermont practitioner.

Virginia

Virginia Board of Bar Examiners
700 East Main St.
Richmond, Va. 23219
(804) 786-7623

Must be resident at time of application and continuing through examination.

Attorneys may be admitted without examination from states which grant similar privileges to Virginia applicants. Must have practiced for five years immediately preceding application. Must be resident at time of application and state intent to maintain a practice in Virginia. All information regarding admission on motion including applications may be obtained from the Clerk of the Supreme Court, Supreme Court of Virginia, P.O. Box 1315, Richmond, Va. 23210.

Washington

Admissions Department
505 Madison St.
Seattle, Wash. 98104
(206) 622-6054

Must be resident at time of admission. Check with Committee for other specifics.

Exam required. Provision for legal-services lawyers.

West Virginia
Board of Law Examiners
E. 404 Capital Building
Charleston, W. Va. 25305
(304) 348-7815

Must be resident thirty days prior to exam.

Must have been a resident of West Virginia for thirty days prior to administration and actively practiced law for five years in another jurisdiction. Special rules for law teachers and legal-services lawyers.

Wisconsin
Board of State Bar Commissioners
231 East, State Capitol
Madison, Wis. 53702
(608) 266-1887

No examinations required of graduates of approved Wisconsin Law Schools. For others, residency is required. However the board will permit a nonresident to take the exam if applicant furnishes a letter from a Wisconsin firm giving an employment commitment. In such case, applicant must become resident within sixty days after exam.

May be admitted without examination if resident and have actively practiced or taught law five out of the last eight years.

Wyoming
State Board of Law Examiners of Wyoming
P. O. Box 3388
Cheyenne, Wyo. 82001
(307) 632-9061

Must be resident at time of exam and for minimum of six months prior to actual admission.

Must be resident for minimum of six months prior to application. Must have practiced law for five of the preceding eight years.

Appendix B
Federal Statutes Authorizing the Award of Attorneys' Fees

Federal Contested Election Act, 2 U.S.C. 396

A candidate for the House of Representatives may contest the election result and claim a right to the seat involved by litigating the claim before a Committee of the House. The Committee may allow reimbursement of any party's reasonable expenses, including reasonable attorneys' fees, upon a verified application for expenses with supporting vouchers and receipts.

Freedom of Information Act, 5 U.S.C. 552(a) (4) (E)

Any person requesting government records may bring suit in the District of Columbia to challenge the refusal to provide such documents. If plaintiff substantially prevails in such a suit, the court may assess against the United States reasonable attorneys' fees.

Privacy Act, 5 U.S.C. 552a(g)(3)(B)

Any person may bring a civil action in a District Court for damages when an agency fails to amend an individual's record as requested or fails to maintain fair and accurate records concerning the individual. If plaintiff substantially prevails in the suit, the court may assess a reasonable attorneys' fee against the United States, in addition to any award for damages.

Packers and Stockyards Act, 7 U.S.C. 219 (f)

A complainant who has received an award for damages from the Secretary of Agriculture against a stockyard owner, market agency, or dealer for violation of the Act may sue in District Court if the damages are not paid within one year. If the plaintiff prevails, the court may allow recovery of a reasonable attorneys' fee.

Perishable Agricultural Commodities Act, 7 U.S.C. 499g(b), (c)

A complainant who has received an order for award of damages from the Secretary of Agriculture against a dealer for violating the Act may sue in District Court if the damages are not paid within three years. If the plaintiff prevails, the court may allow recovery of a reasonable attorneys' fee. Either party adversely affected by a reparation order of the Secretary may appeal the order within 30 days in District Court; the appellant may be allowed a reasonable attorneys' fee if he prevails.

Agricultural Unfair Trade Practices Act, 7 U.S.C. 2305(a), (c)

An aggrieved party may sue an agricultural products handler in District Court either for damages or injunctive relief from substantial violations of the Act (e.g., coercion or discrimination against certain producers). If plaintiff prevails, a reasonable attorneys' fee may be allowed.

Plant Variety Act, 7 U.S.C. 2565

Developers of novel plants may be granted plant variety protection certificates ("plant patents"). The owner of such a certificate may sue for infringement, asking either for damages or injunctive relief. In exceptional cases, the court may award reasonable attorneys' fees to the prevailing party.

Bankruptcy Act, 11 U.S.C. 104(a (1)

This section of the Act covers voluntary and involuntary bankruptcy, and gives a priority for payment out of the estate of actual and necessary costs of preserving the estate. A single reasonable attorneys' fee may be allowed to the petitioning creditors in involuntary cases or reasonable attorneys' fees may be allowed to the bankrupt in voluntary cases.

——11 U.S.C. 205(c) (12)

This section of the Act covers reorganization of railroads involved in interstate commerce. The District Court may make allowance out of the debtor's estate for actual and reasonable expenses, including reasonable attorneys' fees, incurred in connection with the proceedings by parties in interest or the reorganization managers.

——11 U.S.C. 641

This section of the Act covers corporate reorganizations. The court may allow reimbursement for reasonable attorneys' fees incurred by trustees, officers, petitioning creditors, and the debtor in the proceeding.

——11 U.S.C. 642

This section of the Act covers corporation reorganizations. The court may allow reimbursement for reasonable attorneys' fees incurred by other parties interested (except the SEC) in the proceeding.

——11 U.S.C. 643

This section of the Act covers corporate reorganizations. The court may allow reimbursement for reasonable attorneys' fees incurred by stockholders or creditors who successfully propose or object to a reorganization plan for the debtor.

——11 U.S.C. 644

This section of the Act covers corporate bankruptcy. It covers individual suits against a debtor and allows compensation for reasonable attorneys' fees incurred by any party entitled to compensation in the bankruptcy proceeding.

Federal Credit Union Act, 12 U.S.C. 1786 (o)

This Act covers proceedings against federally insured credit unions. The District Court may award any party reasonable attorneys' fees.

Bank Holding Company Act, 12 U.S.C. 1975

This Act prohibits tying arrangements that require bank customers to obtain additional services from bank holding companies or their subsidiaries. Any person injured in their business or property by reason of such arrangements may sue in District Court and recover treble damages, plus costs of suit, including reasonable attorneys' fees.

Clayton Act, 15 U.S.C. 15

Any person injured in his business or property by reason of any act forbidden by the antitrust laws may sue and recover treble damages, plus costs of suit, including reasonable attorneys' fees.

Unfair Competition Act (FTC), 15 U.S.C. 72

This Act prohibits unfair competition by forbidding the importing or selling of articles at less than their market value or wholesale price. Persons injured in their business or property by reason of such violations may sue and recover treble damages, plus costs of suit, including reasonable attorneys' fees.

Securities Act of 1933, 15 U.S.C. 77(k) (e)

Any person acquiring for value a security for which a false registration statement has been filed with the Securities and Exchange Commission may sue for damages. The District Court may order payment of reasonable attorneys' fees on motion of either party, if the court believes the suit or defense to have been without merit.

Trust Indenture Act, 15 U.S.C. 77www(a)

A person making misleading statements in documents required to be filed under the Act may be sued for damages by any person who sold or purchased a security issued under the indenture. The District Court may assess reasonable attorneys' fees against either party litigant, having due regard to the merits and good faith of the suit or defense.

Securities Exchange Act of 1934, 15 U.S.C. 78(i) (e)

Any person who purchases a security at a price that was affected by violations of the Act may sue the violator for damages. The District Court may assess reasonable attorneys' fees against either party litigant.

——15 U.S.C. 78(r) (a)

A person who makes a false or misleading statement in documents required to be filed under the Act may be sued for damages by a person purchasing a security at a price affected by such statement. The District Court may assess reasonable attorneys' fees against either party litigant.

Jewelers Hall-Mark Act, 15 U.S.C. 298 (b), (c) & (d)

A jewelry trade association, competitor, or customer of a jeweler who violates the Act by falsely stamping gold or silver may sue for damages or injunctive relief. The prevailing party may recover reasonable attorneys' fees.

Truth-in-Lending Act (Fair Credit Billing Amendments), 15 U.S.C. 1640(a)

A creditor who fails to disclose information required to be disclosed under the Act or who engages in unfair billing practices may be sued either by an individual or in a class action. Successful plaintiffs may recover reasonable attorneys' fees in addition to damages.

Fair Credit Reporting Act, 15 U.S.C. 1681(n)

A credit reporting agency or user of credit information about a person that willfully fails to comply with the requirements of the Act may be sued by that person for actual and punitive damages. If plaintiff prevails, a reasonable attorneys' fee may be recovered.

Consumer Product Safety Act, 15 U.S.C. 2072

Any person sustaining an injury by reason of any knowing violation of a consumer product safety rule or order of the Consumer Product Safety Commission may sue for damages, and, if successful, recover reasonable attorneys' fees.

———15 U.S.C. 2073

This Act allows private enforcement of consumer product safety rules by permitting any person to sue for injunctive relief. A plaintiff may elect to recover a reasonable attorneys' fee by a demand in the complaint, in which case the court will award fees to the prevailing party.

Federal Trade Improvements Act (Amendments), 15 U.S.C. 2310(a) (5) (d) (2)

This Act sets federal minimum standards for warranties. Any consumer damaged due to a failure of a supplier, warrantor, or service contractor to comply with obligations under the Act may sue for damages. If a plaintiff prevails, a reasonable attorneys' fee (based on actual time expended) will be allowed, unless the District Court determines an award of fees is inappropriate.

Copyright Act, 17 U.S.C. 116

Any party may be allowed recovery of reasonable attorneys' fees in any action for infringement of copyright (except suits against the United States).

Organized Crime Control Act of 1970, 18 U.S.C. 1964(c)

This Act forbids the investment in enterprises engaged in interstate commerce of income acquired by racketeering or the collection of unlawful debts. Any person injured in business or property by reason of a violation of the Act may sue for treble damages and, if successful, recover a reasonable attorneys' fee.

Education Amendments of 1972, 20 U.S.C. 1617

This Act is designed to improve the quality of education, especially for minority students. A suit for discrimination may be brought against any state or local education agency. The court may allow an award of reasonable attorneys' fees to the prevailing party.

APPENDIX B

Mexican American Treaty Act of 1950, 22 U.S.C. 277d-21

The United States Commissioner on the International Boundary Commission is authorized to compensate property owners and tenants for loss or damage incurred in the construction or operation of works under his jurisdiction. When rendering an award in favor of any claimant, a reasonable attorneys' fee, not to exceed 10 percent of the amount awarded, may be allowed.

International Claims Settlement Act, 22 U.S.C. 1623(f)

When the Foreign Claims Commission makes an award under the claims agreements of the United States (e.g., for nationalization of property), it may allow attorneys' fees, not to exceed 10 percent of the amount awarded.

Federal Tort Claims Act, 28 U.S.C. 2678

This Act waives a portion of the sovereign immunity of the United States and permits certain claims for money damages against the United States. If a plaintiff prevails, or if the case is settled, part of the award may be allowed for reasonable attorneys' fees, not to exceed a certain percentage of the amount awarded.

Norris-LaGuardia Act, 29 U.S.C. 107(e)

This Act requires a complainant seeking an injunction in a labor dispute to post a surety for compensation of any loss which may be sustained by those enjoined. If it is determined that a temporary restraining order or injunction was issued erroneously, the person enjoined may recover costs, including reasonable attorneys' fees, for the expense of defending against the erroneous order.

Fair Labor Standards Act, 29 U.S.C. 216(b)

This Act subjects employers who violate it to liability for unpaid minimum or overtime wages and an equal amount in liquidated damages. If a plaintiff prevails, the District Court must allow reasonable attorneys' fees to be paid by the defendant in addition to the award.

Employees Retirement Income Security Act, 29 U.S.C. 1132(g)*

This Act allows participants, beneficiaries, or fiduciaries of retirement programs to institute suits for relief and recovery against the program. The District Court may allow costs, including a reasonable attorneys' fee, to either party, at its discretion.

Labor Management Reporting and Disclosure Act, 29 U.S.C. 431(c)

Under the Act, labor organizations are required to submit certain reports to the United States. The organization is subject to suit by a member to allow inspection of the records and accounts underlying such reports. In such suits, the District Court may award a successful plaintiff costs, including reasonable attorneys' fees.

——29 U.S.C. 501(b)

This section permits members of labor organizations to sue officers of such organizations for breach of fiduciary duties if the governing body of the organization, upon request of the member, refuses to sue to recover damages against the officers. Damages, an accounting, or any other appropriate relief may be awarded by the court, and a reasonable amount of the recovery in any such action may be used to pay the fees of plaintiff's counsel.

Longshoremen and Harbor Workers Compensation Act, 33 U.S.C. 928

This Act allows payment for any legal services rendered in connection with a longshoreman's or harbor worker's claim for compensation for injuries.

Water Pollution Prevention and Control Act, 33 U.S.C. 1365(d)

This Act allows citizen suits to enforce a water effluent standard of the Environmental Protection Agency or state order regarding such standard. The court may award costs, including reasonable attorneys' fees, to any party whenever it determines such an award to be appropriate.

---

* Replaced the Welfare and Pension Plan Disclosure Act, 29 U.S.C. 308(c).

APPENDIX B

Ocean Dumping Act, 33 U.S.C. 1415(g) (4)

This Act prohibits ocean dumping without permit from the Environmental Protection Agency. It allows citizen suits to enforce the Act against violators. The District Court may award costs, including reasonable attorneys' fees, to either party when it determines such an award to be appropriate.

Deepwater Ports Act of 1974, 33 U.S.C. 1515

This Act regulates the activities within deepwater ports and it requires a license issued by the Secretary of Transportation for operations or construction in such a port. It allows citizen suits to enforce the Act. The District Court may award costs, including reasonable attorneys' fees, to either party when it determines such an award to be appropriate.

Patent Infringement Act, 35 U.S.C. 285

In patent infringement suits under the Act, the court may, in exceptional cases, award reasonable attorneys' fees to the prevailing party.

Servicemen's Group Life Insurance Act, 38 U.S.C. 784(g)

This Act allows suits to be filed in District Court in disputes over claims relating to National Service Life Insurance or U.S. Government Life Insurance. The court, as part of its judgment, shall determine and allow attorneys' fees (not to exceed 10 percent of the award in most circumstances) to the prevailing party.

Servicemen's Readjustment Act, 38 U.S.C. 1822(b)

This Act allows suits for treble damages against those who sell real property to a veteran in excess of its reasonable value, if the property was paid for in part with government loan funds. The court may award reasonable attorneys' fees to a successful plaintiff.

Veterans Benefit Act, 38 U.S.C. 3404(c)

This act allows the Veterans' Administrator to recognize attorneys authorized to prosecute veterans' claims before the Veterans' Administration, and to allow a maximum attorneys' fee of $10 to be deducted from each claim.

Safe Drinking Water Act, 42 U.S.C. 300j-8(d)

This Act establishes national drinking water standards, and allows citizens suits to enforce them. The District Court may award costs, including reasonable attorneys' fees, to any party, whenever it determines such an award to be appropriate.

Social Security Act (Amendments of 1965), 42 U.S.C. 406(b)

This Act covers suits for Social Security claims. The court may allow up to 25 percent of the total award as an attorneys' fee for successful plaintiffs.

Clean Air Act (Amendments of 1970), 42 U.S.C. 1857h-2

This Act contains provisions for clean air emission standards, and allows citizen suits to enforce such standards or an order of the Environmental Protection Agency respecting such standards. The court may award costs, including reasonable attorneys' fees, to any party when the court determines such an award to be appropriate.

Voting Rights Act, 42 U.S.C. 1973(e)

A reasonable attorneys' fee may be awarded to the prevailing party in any action or proceeding to enforce the voting guarantees of the Fourteenth or Fifteenth Amendments.

Civil Rights Act of 1967, Title II, 42 U.S.C. 2000a-3

This Title covers suits for discrimination or segregation in public accommodations. The court may allow costs, including reasonable attorneys' fees, to any prevailing party, except the United States.

Civil Rights Act of 1964, Title VII, 42 U.S.C. 2000e-5

This Title prohibits racial, ethnic, religious, or sexual discrimination in employment practices. It allows suit by an aggrieved person who files a charge with the Equal Employment Opportunity Commission which is dismissed

APPENDIX B

or in which a conciliation agreement is not entered. The court may allow a prevailing party, except the United States or the Commission, to recover costs, including reasonable attorneys' fees.

Fair Housing Act of 1968, 42 U.S.C. 3612(c)

This Act prohibits discrimination in the sale and rental of housing and allows suit to enforce rights under the Act. The court may award real and punitive damages or grant equitable relief, and may allow a prevailing plaintiff to recover costs, including reasonable attorneys' fees.

Noise Control Act of 1972, 42 U.S.C. 4911(d)

This Act sets noise control standards, and allows citizen suits to enforce such standards. The court may award costs, including reasonable attorneys' fees, to any party when it determines such an award to be appropriate.

Railway Labor Act, 45 U.S.C. 153(p)

This Act establishes the National Railroad Adjustment Board's jurisdiction over disputes between rail labor organizations and rail carriers. Section (p) allows suits by claimants to whom the Board has ordered compensation when the carrier fails to comply with the order within the time limit established by the Board. If the petitioner ultimately prevails, he shall be awarded a reasonable attorneys' fee, to be taxed and collected as part of the costs of the suit.

The Civil Rights Attorney's Fees Award Act of 1976, 42 U.S.C. 1988

In any action or proceeding to enforce a provision of Sections 1981, 1982, 1983, 1985 and 1986 of Title 42, or of Title IX of Public Law 92-318 (20 U.S.C. 1681), or in any civil action or proceeding by or on behalf of the United States to enforce a provision of the Internal Revenue Code or of Title VI of the 1964 Civil Rights Act, the Court in its discretion may allow a reasonable attorney's fee to the prevailing party other than the United States.